# Fighting for Their Lives

*Inside the Experience of Capital Defense Attorneys*

Susannah Sheffer

Vanderbilt University Press
Nashville

© 2013 by Vanderbilt University Press
Nashville, Tennessee 37235
All rights reserved
First printing 2013

This book is printed on acid-free paper.
Manufactured in the United States of America

Library of Congress Cataloging-in-Publication Data on file

LC control number 2012032701
LC classification number KF9227.C2S54 2013
Dewey class number 345.73'0773—dc23

ISBN 978-0-8265-1910-8 (cloth)
ISBN 978-0-8265-1911-5 (paperback)
ISBN 978-0-8265-1912-2 (e-book)

# Fighting for Their Lives

# CONTENTS

# ACKNOWLEDGMENTS

Without quite knowing what it might be like to do so, twenty attorneys gave me their time, their trust, and their best effort at self-examination. My gratitude to them is profound and my respect beyond measure.

Margaret Vandiver and Dick Burr each offered crucial early support for the project and a nourishing belief in my ability to carry it out. I am inspired by the standard Margaret sets as an interviewer and thinker and by the compassion Dick brings to everything he does, including his reading of my earlier work. I marvel at the path from that reading to this writing.

In my travels, Bobby and Leslee Paul were ideal hosts in Atlanta, rivaled only by Jennifer and Walter Long in Austin.

In the later stages of work, Robin Maher at the American Bar Association's Death Penalty Representation Project graciously answered my factual and historical questions. Susan Bandes offered helpful comments and the pleasure of shared fascinations. Michael Ames at Vanderbilt University Press is the kind of editor writers dream of finding: thoughtful, responsive, and an advocate for a book's heart and soul.

Conversations form the core of this book, and many conversations have enriched its development. Throughout, I have been grateful for the chance to discuss psychology, trauma, and the human condition with Edith Ackermann, Marilyn Armour, Peter Bergson, Amos Blanton, Charlie and Judy Brice, Gene and Sue Burkart, Bobby Dellelo, David Elvin, Rita Falbel, Pat Farenga, Joy Gaines-Friedler, Francine Goldenhar, Dan Grego, Dwight Harrison, Ron Honberg, Roget Lockard, Diane Neal, Peg Padnos, Virginia Raymond, Lowell Rubin, Sajay Samuel, Mali Sastri, David Schwartz, James Staub, and my colleagues at North Star.

Ira Sharkey taught me a whole lot of what I know about creating a space in which to explore emotional experience, and his insight and sensibility are woven into these pages.

My colleagues at Murder Victims' Families for Human Rights, individually and collectively, have provided intellectual and emotional sustenance, sharp insight, and bizarre inside jokes. For over a decade I have learned from Renny Cushing and Kate Lowenstein about the impact of violent loss, how to write and talk about it with care, and how to keep working for a better world. Priscilla Caputo, my reliable optimist, has been thoughtful and supportive of every challenge, from the mundane to the profound.

My friends Natalie Rusk, Victoria Olsen, Michael Nicholas, Jeri Bayer, Jen Konieczny, Carrie Kline, and my cousin Elinor Brook have heard so much about this project that they must feel vicariously a part of it. No brief acknowledgment can convey how each of these people has enriched my life and work. Likewise, my parents Ethel and Isaiah Sheffer, who have taught me so much through their own lives and work, were enthusiastic about the project from the start and have readily supplied ideas, support, and inspiration.

The book is far better than it would have been if Amanda Bergson-Shilcock had not read and commented on every line (except this one). A long time ago, I was the one mentoring Amanda; now she is my prose's toughest critic and fiercest champion, and my dear friend.

To describe Walter Long as a consultant to the project would vastly underestimate how vital his involvement has been from the beginning. I would not have thought it, felt it, or undertaken it if not for Walter's own interest in this territory. There would be no book without his openness and his readiness to think with me about every detail.

My husband Aaron Falbel, another astute early reader of the manuscript, finds ways to make me collapse with laughter at least once a day, understands my need to hit the road periodically for projects like this one, and is always, always the reason I look forward to coming home.

# CHAPTER I

# The Challenges of Capital Defense

THE FIRST TIME one of his clients was executed, Adam had been work-ing on the case only six weeks. By the time he was asked to help, almost all the available strategies had been exhausted and the execution date was looming. For those six weeks he lived on three hours of sleep a night and thought of almost nothing but the legal petition he was preparing. "The only way I can describe it," he says, "is that I would get up in the morning and there was an elephant on my chest."

Adam knew the odds were against him; he'd known that from the moment he agreed to take the case so late in the game. But he still remem-bers the night of the execution, the strange desolation of being on the phone with the colleague who had begged him to take the case in the first place and just crying together. He remembers telling himself, "I had done everything I could do. I couldn't give another ounce of effort."

By the time Adam tells me this story, he has been a capital defense attorney for over two decades. He has learned and relearned how to give every ounce of effort for a client facing execution—and how to remind himself that he's done as much as is humanly possible.

It's persuasive, and I don't doubt him, but still I ask, "Do you ever *not* feel that? Do you ever have questions about whether there was something else you could have done?"

Adam nods: *oh yeah.* He begins describing a morning not long after he had lost his third client in three years to execution. Sitting in his kitchen drinking coffee, he happened to hear a radio news story about a boy who had wandered away from his family on a hiking trail. It was late fall, the nights were getting colder, and the search team understood that they didn't have much time.

Adam looks at me to see if I can guess where this story's going. I can already picture the exhaustion and fear in the rescuers' faces by the third night, when, as Adam tells it, they finally found the boy's body in a cove several yards from the main trail.

Alone in his kitchen, getting ready to go to work, Adam was overtaken by sobs. "I listen to the rescue guy explain that he thought they had looked everywhere," Adam recalls, the memory thickening his voice. "And out loud in the kitchen I say to myself, *what was wrong with him?*"

Never mind the many possible ways to see this story. That morning, for Adam, it had its own cruel logic: if the rescuer had the power to save the boy, then it must have been the rescuer's incapacity that failed him. Adam doesn't need to make any transition as he switches back to talking about the death penalty; the analogy is palpable.

"I mean, you know, intellectually, that the execution is not your fault. But your job is to save this person's life! And you *didn't do it.*" He pauses and looks at me. "No matter how much you tell yourself that you've done everything you could do, your job was to save his life and you didn't."

In the landscape of the death penalty, capital defense attorneys stand in a very particular spot. Like those who testify at legislative hearings, hold vigils, or organize conferences promoting death penalty abolition, these attorneys are working in opposition to capital punishment. But although many may call for an end to the death penalty, only the capital defenders are specifically charged with the task of stopping, and have the legal tools that might be able to stop, each particular impending execution, over and over again.

An individual execution may be cited as significant because of the particular issues it represents, or it may pass largely unnoticed by the wider community. For capital defenders, however, the political utility of focusing or not focusing on any one execution is not foremost in their minds. However sympathetic or unsympathetic the client, however illustrative or not illustrative of some problem within the death penalty process, each one demands an all-out effort. Each one not only represents but actually *is* a life or death matter, and the battle must be fought right now, no waiting for a better time.

While the death penalty debate rages on, with arguments mounted pro and con, within the prison cell a person's life is in the balance. This need is urgent, specific, compelling: this individual will either die tonight or he won't. The capital defenders are not just *watching to see* what will happen; they are the ones who might actually be able to change the outcome. If you are a capital defender with a client under death warrant, that piece of paper means a date has been set for the taking of that individual's life, and if there's any way to stop that from happening, you're the one who must find it.

If the execution happens anyway, what does that mean to the attorney who tried so hard to prevent it? Because a capital defender stands in a unique relationship to an execution, the event demands a personal reckoning that it does not demand of anyone else. *Your job was to save his life.* Strip away the legal language and this is what it is.

What is this like? That's what I wanted to know. Not what it's like in the courtroom or in the offices of a capital habeas unit where attorneys are writing pleadings late into the night, rich and textured though those stories are. My greater curiosity was, what is it like for capital defenders in the middle of the night, in the pit of the stomach, in their last visits or phone calls with clients who are about to be taken to the execution chamber, in the mornings after, in their lives with their families, in their dreams and flashbacks and quiet moments alone?

I arrived at this particular curiosity after fifteen years of immersion in other *what is it like?* explorations regarding the death penalty, criminal justice, and how people harm and are harmed. I had collaborated on the memoir of a former prisoner convicted of a violent crime. I had for years visited another man serving a life sentence. I had served on the staff of an organization working in opposition to the death penalty, with a membership comprising families of murder victims and families of people who have been executed. All this involved challenging a cascade of common assumptions: that prisoners are unrepentant monsters, that murder victims' family members unanimously favor the death penalty, and that the death penalty is society's best response in the aftermath of a murder. Whether I was asking about daily life in the isolation unit of a maximum security prison or about how the murder of a loved one devastates a family, my questions were always about how people are affected by their experience, how they come to understand or make sense of it, how they are by turns fragile and resilient, and how, much of the time, they find a way to carry on. Turning my attention to capital defenders was in many ways the culmination of a decade and a half of focus on human subjectivity within the context of social policies that fall under the broad banner of criminal justice.

Personal conversations initially sparked my curiosity about capital defenders. Informal exchanges with a few attorneys I knew through my death penalty work gave me a glimpse of the complexity of their experience. I began to get a feel for the internal tensions beneath their extraordinary dedication and commitment, and the toll the work might be taking on them even though they couldn't imagine doing anything else. I decided to approach them with an idea: I would conduct confidential interviews with capital defenders, focusing on their emotional experience, and then write about what I learned.

Their immediate response to the idea contained a mix of curiosity and resistance that I would repeatedly encounter as the project went forward, and that was itself as moving and as revealing of the capital defender's experience as anything else. "It's never been looked at in any depth, and maybe the time has come to do it," said one. "Despite the feeling in my stomach that I get when I think about it, I believe this is important and I will talk to you."

Without the early support of these respected capital defenders who implicitly vouched for me when referring me to others, it would have been tough, maybe even impossible, to set up the rest of the interviews. Having this essential endorsement, I set out to contact additional attorneys, who in turn referred me to others.

I knew early on that I was interested in attorneys experienced in the post-conviction stage of capital defense—the end stage, often occurring many years after the original murder trial, conviction, and death sentence. By this point in a capital case, trial and direct appeal advocacy by other attorneys has yielded no relief, in the legal sense, for the defendant, who is now on death row. Post-conviction defense attorneys enter the case to provide a final firewall of protection, reviewing the record and reinvestigating the case to determine if the defendant received a constitutionally fair trial, and, if not, to try to do something about it. More often than they would like, they find themselves working under the pressure of a looming execution date—a threat that earlier defense counsel didn't have to face.

Though Hollywood has popularized the image of attorneys racing against the clock to get a last-minute reprieve, and real death penalty cases do sometimes include dramatic stays of execution, the actual work of post-conviction litigation is often more prosaic. "I think for a lot of people, post-conviction is not even [what they picture when they think of] lawyering," one of my interviewees speculated. "We don't even get to court very often. I get a record, I write a document, I FedEx it to a court, I get back an order saying, *you lose*. I could be doing it from Mars. It's still litigation, but to the outside observer, it's like, Where is the court? Where is the drama?"

Of course, when a post-conviction attorney does get to court, it's sometimes to the highest court in the land, as capital cases at this stage are sometimes heard by US Supreme Court justices. But for the most part, the drama of post-conviction legal work has a different look to it. Reading the record, investigating the case, writing the document—all of this may appear comparatively subdued, but it is in fact infused with great intellectual, emotional, and even physical intensity. Adam's story of working with little sleep under enormous deadline pressure is typical.

In post-conviction litigation, the attorney raises issues that were not addressed earlier, either because previous defense attorneys did not raise them or because prosecuting attorneys prevented them from being raised. Post-conviction involves looking at ways in which the client's constitutional rights may have been violated by something that was done, or not done, at an earlier stage of the process. The most common means through which the attorney does this is by petitioning for a writ of habeas corpus, which is the legal mechanism by which a prisoner can challenge the basis of his confinement.

As the attorneys interviewed here describe, habeas's roots in constitutional law make this stage of capital litigation particularly intellectually engaging. For the same reason, habeas litigation can be fueled by—or can awaken—a strong drive to correct injustice and protect fundamental rights. "Habeas is the system's way of monitoring itself," is how one attorney explained it to me. "In our system of law, we give an individual one chance at a fair trial. But if that didn't happen the first time, and it can be shown that it didn't happen, then habeas is a way of correcting that."

All of this is especially urgent when a person's life is at stake and when it seems highly likely that if certain issues had been raised, or if the conduct of key players had been different, this client might have received a sentence other than death. Did the client's trial attorney fail to find out about and introduce evidence that would have made it possible for the jury to acquit or to give a life sentence? Did the state withhold crucial evidence? Did a juror harbor a prejudice or have a personal association with one of the state's witnesses that was not revealed at the time of trial? Did an eyewitness lie on the stand or change her mind about what she thought she had seen?

There are a lot of possibilities, and so post-conviction work involves not only meticulous record review and voluminous brief writing but also vigorous investigation into the facts supporting the prosecution's case and into the life history of the client—information that might have led to very different trial outcomes had the investigation been undertaken earlier. Learning what *wasn't* done and what wasn't previously introduced can ignite in the post-conviction attorney a fierce desire to correct that omission now.

But as we will also see, overturning a death sentence is much harder than preventing it from being handed down in the first place. Habeas might be a critically important built-in monitoring system, but in practice attorneys find that stopping an oncoming train is vastly more difficult than blocking that train from ever leaving the station. The attorneys feel the situation as urgent: a life is being threatened. But the threat is so particular and its impact so hidden from public view that outsiders may wonder at the effort or even believe that if the train is already en route, there must be good reason for it.

In embarking on an exploration of capital defenders' emotional experience, I was interested in the post-conviction stage because its drama is located not in spellbinding courtroom arguments but in the nature of the litigation and the urgency of the impending threat to the client. I wanted to know how attorneys live with that urgent threat and how they are affected by the myriad losses they inevitably experience—of the case and of the client they have come to know and often to care for very deeply. In fact, I specifically decided that I wanted to interview only capital defenders who had lost at least one client to execution. As it turned out, this was a conservative criterion. Working for two or three decades in the "death belt" of the South, holding primary responsibility for several cases and varying degrees of involvement with many more, most of these experienced capital defenders had lost not just one client but five, or ten, or twenty.

Just a handful of states have been responsible for well over half the executions in the US during what is called the modern death penalty era (since 1976), and the overwhelming majority of those states are in the South. So, rather than aiming to represent a range of states within the US as a whole, I wanted to interview attorneys who have worked where executions have been most common. Over their long careers, several of the attorneys I spoke with have worked in a variety of geographical locations and have also sometimes represented clients in states other than the one where they primarily live and work. Though I traveled to interview attorneys in five different states, collectively this group has worked on capital cases in Arkansas, California, Georgia, Florida, Louisiana, Mississippi, North Carolina, Oklahoma, Pennsylvania, South Carolina, Texas, and Virginia. Of the twenty interviewees, six are women and fourteen are men. Their length of time practicing capital defense ranges from eight to thirty-two years, with the average about nineteen years. All the interviews were conducted between January and November 2010.

These twenty interviewees are among the relatively small group of defense attorneys in the United States who have chosen to work in an area where the need for skilled and dedicated representation vastly outstrips the number of attorneys who are qualified and available. The American Bar Association's (ABA) Death Penalty Representation Project estimates that hundreds of prisoners are on death row in the United States without any legal representation at all. Capital post-conviction offices, some publicly funded and many operating as private non-profits, provide much of the available experienced representation, and these offices are often deluged with more requests than they can fulfill. Other attorneys work at firms that allow them to focus on capital litigation, and some have set up private practices with this focus.

None of the attorneys interviewed were among the substantial number also recruited from corporate law firms by the ABA death penalty project to provide pro bono representation for inmates facing death sentences in places where no other attorney could be found, which is a common problem. Gone are the days of the Capital Resource Centers, through which federal funds enabled attorneys who specialized in capital defense to represent clients themselves and also to provide extensive mentoring and guidance to other attorneys who agreed to take cases. Several of the attorneys interviewed worked at one of those centers before Congress eliminated their funding in 1995.

Capital defense attorneys who have been practicing since the 1990s, as have most of my interviewees, recall that period as a watershed moment when the conditions surrounding death penalty litigation worsened significantly. The closing of the resource centers had a big impact, and the passage of the federal Antiterrorism and Effective Death Penalty Act (AEDPA) in 1996 imposed severe restrictions on prisoners' ability to challenge their death sentences, most notably by limiting the timeframe in which a prisoner can petition for federal review of a case and, once a petition is filed, the issues the federal court may consider. Repeatedly the attorneys I interviewed lamented the ways in which these procedural changes have made it harder, or even sometimes impossible, for them to raise issues they consider critical.

I was interested in exploring both the motivation and the burden that this context creates. What is it like to work within this climate of urgent need and scarcity of resources, all while navigating a dense thicket of procedural rules and restrictions? What does it mean to have chosen, rather than simply been assigned, this kind of work?

Of the attorneys I approached, only two said, essentially, "Good project but I prefer not to participate." But I did often detect the mix of interest and wariness that I alluded to earlier, implicit in some of the first responses to my emails or perceptible as a look in the eyes when we first sat down to speak. What it told me was that an interview with this kind of focus was, above all, unfamiliar. I came to feel that the question of whether to talk about how they are affected by the work—and even whether to examine it in the privacy of their own minds—is a dilemma so intrinsic to the experience of the work that it merits its own consideration, and so I devote Chapter 6 to that question. However, there are a couple of things to say about it now.

One reason for the attorneys' initial ambivalence about focusing on their own emotional experience was a discomfort with putting themselves at the center of the story. They are aware that many do not view the capital defense attorney as the main character in the death penalty drama. As some of the attorneys put it, "I'm not the one who died." That acknowledgment can refer to the executed client, the murder victim to whose death the execution is ostensibly a response, or both. In citing this as a reason not to focus on themselves, these capital defenders were speaking from exactly the "it's not about me" stance that often fuels their dedication, their willingness to give up sleep and time and so much else in service to something else, someone else.

But it's worth asking, in this or any context, whether suffering, or discussion of it, must be a zero-sum exercise. Does an examination of the ways in which any one group is affected by an experience necessarily contain within it the assumption that it is the group *most* affected? Or affected in a way that is qualitatively worse? Does one suffering trump another—or is trumping perhaps not the issue?

I regularly encounter a version of this zero-sum assumption. Those whose activism or advocacy focuses on prisoners, for example, may neglect to take the victims' perspectives into account, while those who focus on victims sometimes speak as if any concern for the defendant's rights or suffering represents a disregard for the victim's. Because my own engagement with the death penalty and related criminal justice issues is rooted in a close look at what both the victims and the perpetrators (and their families) experience, the either/or stance has never made sense to me. Of course I am not alone in having this dual focus; there are many others whose work, in whatever form, encompasses or takes into account multiple experiences, multiple perspectives.

The key question, it seems to me, is not who is most harmed, but *how* are people harmed, and what might anyone do about it? If there's no shortage of pain to go around when terrible tragedies occur, maybe there need not be a scarcity of attention paid to the range of that pain, either. Maybe we—as a society and as individuals—can afford to consider the variety of people who are affected by a societal practice. Maybe we actually have a responsibility to look at those effects.

There's yet another reason to examine the experience of capital defense attorneys. In some ways, to be sure, the work of these death penalty lawyers is unlike any other enterprise, but it also shares something with other high-pressure, emotionally demanding endeavors, specifically those that involve taking on the responsibility of trying to help or even save another person. Even though capital defense differs from other lifesaving efforts—perhaps most obviously because defense attorneys are subject to public prejudice that the lives of their clients are not worth fighting for—there is also some powerful overlap. Members of the various helping professions will likely find much to identify with in the motivations and experiences of these attorneys. The questions capital defenders confront in their distinct context are questions that others in the helping professions face as well: How much of the responsibility for saving someone, or righting a wrong, falls on any one individual's shoulders? How does such responsibility affect those who carry it? What responsibility do helpers have toward each other and does society have toward them?

Whether it's treating patients in an emergency room or staffing a suicide hotline or rescuing victims of a natural disaster, some people are required and must be willing to perform extraordinary and difficult tasks where adrenaline runs high and loss is all too common. We don't ask, as often as we might, what it is like for the human beings who do these kinds of things—both what the work takes from them and what it gives. Conducting these interviews was my way of asking.

> When I got your email, I laughed to myself. You wanted to know about my experience and I said to myself, no one wants to know about that—even my husband doesn't want to know much about that!

> Nobody ever really asks. Or they ask, but I always assume they're not really interested, they're just a little bit interested.

> No one has ever asked me these questions before. This is not what people usually want to know about.

> I would guess there's probably a very deeply repressed need to tell our own story.

Amidst comments about being unaccustomed to talking about their own experiences, I also heard comments like these, suggesting to me that underneath or alongside the unfamiliarity there might also be an actual desire to talk at this level. I trusted that desire, laced with ambivalence though it might be. I knew that attorneys who agreed to meet with me were probably agreeing for a constellation of reasons, and I believed that among those reasons might be a curiosity, however muffled, about what it would be like to explore some of this stuff. On the one hand, this is a generous group of people, used to trying to help when help is requested and, in particular, making a strong effort to respond when one of their own colleagues asks (as when some agreed to be interviewed after I had been referred by one of their colleagues). On the other hand, these are also people with more demands on their time and fewer hours of sleep over the course of any month or year than I've ever known. Anyone who wanted to plead busyness in order to decline my request could have reasonably done so. That so many accepted the invitation, and took two or three hours out of jam-packed days, told me something.

Given how relatively new or unfamiliar our conversational territory would be, I felt it was important to conduct the interviews in person rather than by telephone. Later, as I listened and re-listened to the interviews and pored over the transcripts, I felt that much of what transpired would not have happened in the same way over the telephone, nor would I have been able to think and write about it in the same way.

Most of the interviews were held not in the attorneys' offices but in another nearby, comfortable, private location. Some interviewees had specifically told me in advance that they preferred not to meet in their office, and even for those who didn't bring it up, I suspected that an alternate space would be preferable. Free from the office's distractions and competing demands, and less requiring of the attorney's familiar professional persona, a guesthouse or a meeting room at a university seemed to offer a kind of sanctuary, or at least a departure from ordinary daily concerns, that facilitated the kinds of conversations we were having. The few I did meet at their offices tried to create a similar feeling, for example by using a conference room rather than their own office.

I explained at the start that the interviews would be confidential, in that I would use pseudonyms when quoting and would remove the kinds of details that might make it easy to identify the speaker. Most often, these would include details about specific cases or a particular attorney's biography. I explained this to the attorneys before they agreed to the interview and again as we got started. With some, I sensed that this was an essential precondition for their agreeing to talk with me. For others, its value only became fully apparent as they discovered just how unfamiliar the territory was and how surprised they sometimes were by their own responses.

Even if some were initially more concerned about confidentiality than others were, I felt strongly that it was a necessary part of the process for all the interviewees. Capital defenders are used to speaking on the record, whether court or media. For the kinds of conversations we were having, it was essential to establish and maintain a very different framework. As I've begun to suggest here, and as will become even more apparent throughout this book, these attorneys are unaccustomed to speaking about the emotional impact of their work, particularly among themselves. In order to make their reflections available not only to the wider world but also to each other, I had to first assure them that their colleagues and others who knew them personally would not easily recognize them.

I prepared a brief list of questions and topics I wanted to explore, but in the interviews I didn't follow it precisely. The structure was more like a conversation: I listened closely to how they responded and stayed alert to opportunities where we might go deeper, follow the trail further. The only question I asked consistently, at the same point in each interview, was the opening: "How did you get into this work?" I wanted to know, of course— the contextual information, their reflections on their motivations and on the particular draw of capital defense work. But I also wanted to offer a relatively easy question at the outset, one that would involve explaining or recounting a story with which they were largely already familiar.

What was fascinating to experience—and it occurred reliably in each interview, though at different moments—was the switch from this familiar storytelling, an almost perceptible downshifting as they themselves became engaged with the conversation, grew curious about their own answers, and even began to surprise themselves with their words. At the start they might answer a question and then look back at me, waiting for the next one, but after a while I found that if I kept silent when they paused, they would continue with their own reflections. It was almost as if they began to tune into another frequency, one that had been there all along but that they were less likely to attend to in the press of daily demands and their familiar focus on advocating for their clients or the issues that their clients' cases exemplify.

For interviewees coming from a tight and fairly insular world, it can be hard to talk to someone who is such an outsider that it's necessary to explain every reference and assumption. But the converse is also true. It can be equally difficult to speak to others so embedded in that world that they share those same references and assumptions and thus may not think to question them, and moreover may have their own stake in the responses. I believe that my position as both an insider (already engaged in death penalty work) and an outsider (not myself a capital defender) was an advantage.

My position and my promise of confidentiality combined to make possible that tuning to a different frequency, which in turn yielded the material that now fills these pages. While little of the attorneys' outward identity is visible here, which may limit readers' ability to form a distinct picture of any one of them, an important dimension of their experience is now vivid in ways that it has not been before. Perhaps paradoxically, it was necessary to obscure some aspects of their lives and work in order to reveal others. For the opportunity to bring to light one of the unexplored impacts of capital punishment, this seemed to me an exchange well worth making.

Of course, given all this, the attorneys were understandably intrigued by the fact that other capital defenders like themselves had also agreed to be interviewed. "We don't talk about this stuff," one after another explained to me, and yet here they were now, talking. Contemplating this at the end of his interview, one said, "I think there *is* a need to speak the unspeakable."

After so many hours of listening, I came to feel that "the unspeakable," while perhaps referring to aspects of the death penalty—what it is actually like to witness an execution or to speak with clients in their final moments before being taken away—mainly consists of the defender's own internal experience, or the part of it less commonly recognized and considered.

They are right, of course, when they say they are not the center of the story. But they are the center of *a* story, the one about what it is like to work in this particular way, live in this particular way, wrestle with these particular kinds of experiences. This is the story that it has been my great privilege to go after, listen to, assimilate over many weeks and months, and, now, to synthesize and tell.

# CHAPTER 2

# The Motivations

JULIAN IS TELLING me about the first death penalty case he worked on. He hadn't yet taken the bar exam; he was a law student helping out, as law students who show any interest in capital defense are often recruited to do.

"I was so enraged by what I saw of the process," he says, his voice enlivened by the memory. A lot of the rage has to do with his sense that no one seemed to care how much was at stake. The nonchalance of the other players in the courtroom drama, the flimsiness of the evidence being used to sentence a man to death, the pettiness of some of the rules—all of this is still vivid to him, and maddening.

"Realizing how manifestly violent and insensitive and unjust the system was, that pulled me in," Julian explains. "I said, I can't help but fight this."

"Did it feel fightable?"

"It didn't matter! I mean, it was just wrong. Just wrong."

On first hearing, there's nothing personal in this declaration. It's a statement about social injustice that does not seem, on the surface, to say anything about the individual who has chosen to step in and make an effort to right that wrong. Yet as I listen to Julian describe what he has seen, I am also listening for clues to the man who identifies these particular things as wrong and who feels himself compelled to step in. "I can't help but fight this," he says. Why not? Part of the answer is surely that it needed fighting. But part of the answer, I think to myself, must also lie somewhere in Julian—somewhere in each capital defender I'm speaking with—since plenty of people *can* help but fight this particular battle, or choose to fight something else, or don't go looking for fights in quite the same way.

Later in our interview, Julian talks about other cases and his decision to litigate up to the last possible minute, whatever the actual chances of winning might be.

"It's a matter of principle," he explains.

"Would there be a way to express that principle with a first-person pronoun?" I wonder out loud.

"I don't know. That's an interesting question. I don't think of it with an 'I.' It's just like, This is wrong, it's got to be corrected, what do I do?"

"Hmm, so *there's* the 'I.'"

"Sort of. What needs to be done, and then I do it." He stops to think a minute. Clearly just using the word "I" in the sentence isn't the same as really reflecting on where his own subjectivity comes into the story. I can feel him slowing down, considering the question.

> [My wife] would probably tell you that in times when I'm being that way, I'm just utterly focused and it's sort of like there's no— well, I think I'm telling you more of how I used to be. I think now I've learned to observe myself in the process more than I used to. I think all of us defense attorneys need to learn to do that; we all need to understand better what's going on within us so we can talk more about the "I" you're getting at. But back then, I wouldn't be so conscious of the "I." When I was chasing around looking for witnesses, or doing any number of things, I wasn't thinking about "I." It was like, these are things that need to be done. I'm the agent that's doing them, but I'm not thinking about me, I'm not thinking about what I'm feeling. And at many of these points, it's just been, There's no time left, there's no time to think about it, just do it.

As I listen to him, I think about how hard it is for any of us to see our own motivations clearly and to discern exactly what led us to whatever we end up doing.

"Not everyone does what you do, though," I say to Julian. I don't mean he's better than other people; I just mean that maybe there is always an implicit "I." Maybe there's always an intersection between the work and the person who undertakes it.

Julian is silent for a while. "It's interesting," he says after several moments. "It seems like you're asking about motivation or background, what it is that would make me respond to things that I perceive to be morally wrong. One of the things that just came to mind was the parable of the good Samaritan. The Samaritan refuses to pass by the traveler in the ditch. There's a sense of urgency that these kinds of situations have always engendered in me. There's something in me that refuses to pass by."

Whether or not we want to acknowledge it, there are so many travelers in ditches that, inevitably, we constantly choose when to respond, when to pass by. I remember that as a young adult I sometimes saw societal problems as a battlefield of wounded soldiers, each one needing attention. Standing before that imagined battlefield, I realized it was probably impossible to help all of them, and certainly impossible to help all at once. What are the options? Become frozen by the enormity of the need? Turn away entirely? Or go first to one and then, if one lifetime allows, another and another? But how to pick which one? Maybe try quickly to assess whose need is greatest. Maybe go to the one that you feel most drawn to. Or maybe go to the one that's closest, the one that circumstance seems to have placed right in front of you, so that "motivation" always has some element of chance and is perhaps less about active choice than about what we happen to encounter or stumble into.

Still I say there is some kind of "I," some kind of personal specificity, even in a story of apparently chance encounter. There are many things to do if one is merely interested in doing *something*. Why this? I come back to Julian's "I can't help but fight it." Maybe that's the heart of it. We do in our lives the things we can't help but do—whatever is so compelling to us that when we notice it, we can't look away until we figure out how to do something about what we've seen.

One thing's for sure: capital defense is not on the usual list of childhood ambitions. It wasn't even in the youthful awareness of most of the capital defenders I talked to, most of whom came of age during a period when the death penalty had very little place within the general political or social consciousness. When the US Supreme Court ruled in 1972 that the then-current death penalty statutes were unconstitutional, there hadn't been an execution since 1967.

The landscape changed quickly with the 1976 Supreme Court decisions that upheld many of the new state death penalty statutes that had been passed in the intervening years. Executions resumed in 1977 and increased in frequency in the 1980s and 1990s. By then, the attorneys I interviewed were in college or law school. It was at this point in their lives that most of them began to consider working in this area. Today's anti-death penalty movement has its share of young activists, and it's conceivable that they—or any young person intrigued or outraged by stories of the death penalty in films, books, or news articles—could form an idea, however vague, of one day becoming a death penalty lawyer. But this wasn't something that the attorneys I interviewed thought about until later in their lives. If there is any obvious connection with their childhoods, it comes up in their remarks about being raised to consider the least powerful among us and to think of adult work not only in terms of personal success but also in terms of making a difference in the world.

> I grew up with a tendency to take the side of the underdog and to try to right wrongs. I grew up thinking that what you try to do in life is something that is worthwhile, that makes things better. –Caroline

> I was raised by kind parents who were not terribly politically active or conscious but who were kind people and who made me go to church and probably, although I later felt very alienated from organized religion, I still had the values that were taught to

me—compassion and kindness and acting out of love instead of hatred. Those were the things that I grew up with. –Paul

We were forced to go to Catholic school until I rebelled. I left in second grade! But you know, the way they taught you to deal with the poor and the marginalized, there are some good aspects of the teachings that have stayed with me. Sympathy and empathy for the poor, that's always in me. –Nick

But even this kind of sensibility doesn't always translate to a family's wholehearted support for a young attorney's decision to defend people on death row. "Why'd you bother going to law school if that's what you're going to do?" Nick's mother asked him early on. Some of the attorneys describe their parents as proud of their work, or supportive even if not fully able to understand it, but some speak of outright conflict, as does Simon, who recalls, "My father—this work was completely incomprehensible to him, and we never saw eye to eye. It ended up creating major rifts."

Those who are surprised that a talented law student would choose this area of practice may not recognize that capital defense can be attractive precisely because of the legal skill it requires. "Intellectually it's some of the most challenging legal work you can do," Caroline explains, "because you're dealing with constitutional principles, which flow directly from the Supreme Court, so you're really litigating at a level that you don't when you're doing other kinds of criminal defense work." Caroline's contrast is between capital and other kinds of criminal defense, but the interviewees who contrasted capital defense with other kinds of legal work also emphasized (among other distinctions) that capital defense was more interesting. One attorney said that as a law student he had considered but rejected going into environmental law because "as noble as it is, it's pretty boring." The "nobility" of the work isn't enough by itself; the intellectual challenge and stimulation matter too.

Capital defense also requires lawyers to learn a lot more than the law. Caroline describes it like this:

In the course of representing people in death penalty cases, one of the things that you really need to do is investigate about their lives and to really try to understand how they got from being born to where they are. As you do that, you learn so much not just about this person but about how people do become who they are, what kind of things impact their lives. It's like a whole course in sociology, history. . . . It's really a lesson in life that you get because you're involved in the research.

Pamela remembers an early curiosity about this kind of human story. As a teenager, she read books about crime, wondering how someone could commit terribly violent acts. Then, in law school, which she experienced as "a very prosecution-oriented world," she found herself asking, "Who's going to talk about the people who are ending up in these criminal positions? Because they were people I knew. I grew up in a small town. So you really get a sense of, Everybody started the same, so what makes some end up here and some end up there?"

As I listened to the defenders talk about what drew them to this work, I realized increasingly that it was possible to hear the implicit "I" even in comments that didn't immediately refer to personal motivation. I could hear it, for example, in the way they responded to questions about why the death penalty was the particular social issue that grabbed their attention.

I thought to myself, and it's very vivid in my memory, that there are so many more subtle ways in which we as human beings hurt each other that if we can't get this one, which is so blatant, if we can't fix this one, how in the world are we going to deal with the many more subtle ways in which we injure each other? –Adam

I quickly realized that people who society wanted to kill were clearly the most despised people in the society. And nobody that had any money. So it was that and the notion that if the government could take a life legitimately, that sort of legitimized anything else they did to people short of taking their lives—they could take their money, their houses, cars, they could put them on the street. And so it seemed to me that if we could stop the death penalty, that would somehow in a general sense make things better for people who were otherwise the wretched of the earth. –Paul

I had this image, this understanding, that came to me. I had always wanted to do civil rights work and then I said, you know, *this* is real civil rights work. This is human rights work. This is political and intellectual, where the rubber hits the road, so to speak. So that's what I decided I was going to do. –Roger

These are political and social analyses, of course, but they also begin to suggest the inclinations and temperaments of those doing the analyzing. When people describe a social or political landscape, they reveal as much about themselves through their choice of descriptions as they do about the landscape itself. What specifically do they notice? What grips their attention and imagination? Where do they place their focus? The above comments show us something about these individuals' preoccupations and passions: the way people treat one another, the plight of the "wretched and despised," the relationship between the powerful and the powerless.

Sometimes one's first real exposure to the idea of the death penalty comes through the morning news. Simon was in law school when he heard a radio report of a recent execution.

I remember vividly listening to the radio in the morning and being overwhelmed by the fact that a human being had been exterminated.

*Interesting—you weren't even that close to the issue yet. What was the feeling?*

I think at that time I would put myself in the place of the person. I would sort of imagine what that must be like and would just sort of—there was just something that really tied me up and made me completely frustrated. There's something fundamentally wrong with this. It grabbed me instinctually.

One's reaction to the idea of the death penalty *is* in many ways instinctual, a gut response even in people who have learned a tremendous amount about it legally, politically, and sociologically. Simon's feeling of being "tied up" and "grabbed instinctually" echoes Julian's "I can't help but fight this." Both are describing a visceral recoil at the idea of the death penalty and an instinctive pull toward fighting it that accompanies and maybe even precedes more conscious decisions about what line of work to pursue.

Because he believes society creates the problems that result in death row, Eric feels that "it's my responsibility, it's almost like a social responsibility I have," to work in this area. Labeling something the province of "society" or "the state" could be used as a way to avoid doing anything oneself, but Eric's comment is about feeling a personal identification with the "we" of society. In that sense, he—like the other attorneys who spoke similarly—feels an "I" where others might not.

Typically, the way students spend the summer between their second and third years of law school predicts the way they will spend their careers. Students intern with the firm—or at least the type of firm—that they hope will hire them after graduation, and they get a real-world glimpse of the kind of life and work they're about to embark on. Some law students who intern with capital defenders during that second summer no doubt end up running from the intensity or the grittiness or the long odds that are so intrinsic to the work. But those I spoke with were, perhaps by definition, the ones whose early exposure to capital defense confirmed or ignited the feeling that this was where they belonged.

As a second-summer intern, Gabe found his work with capital defenders so compelling that he became determined to join them when he graduated—so much so that he showed up every day and offered to help out, until eventually he was hired.

"What was the draw?" I ask, thinking that a young man would have to feel that draw pretty strongly to show up regularly even before he had an official job offer.

"It felt meaningful," is Gabe's immediate response. "It felt like something I could do with my law degree that was—that there was a real need for services. I felt really lucky to be able to do this, to be able to use my degree in that way."

Eric describes a similar feeling. After his initial exposure, it didn't take him long to decide that post-conviction capital defense work was what he wanted to pursue. "I think it was because I realized that that group of clients is the most in need of legal services," he explains. "There are, of course, many other worthy things to be doing with a law license, but this group is in the most dire need." Eric says he hadn't known much about the death penalty growing up—"I grew up pretty much apolitically" is how he describes it—but "I'm not a lawyer just to be a lawyer. I want to use my law license to help people in need."

These are lofty words, but sitting with the attorneys as they say these kinds of things, one feels how deeply held, how gut level, the sentiments are. These aren't just catch phrases to write on a job application. Helping clients whom they view as most in need feels like another aspect of what these attorneys "can't help but do."

Elliot tells me that he has never been interested in "siding with the people who have power already." I ask what attracts him to aligning with and working on behalf of those who have less power. He is silent for a few moments.

"It just feels good," he finally answers. "Those are the stories in fiction or nonfiction that move me. The reading that we had at my wedding was of the story in the Bible of the woman who only has two coins and gives away her last coins. You know, at some point it is just a visceral reaction—as I sit here and think of those narratives, I can feel myself tearing up a little bit. And that's not because each individual story is so compelling; it's just that that's the narrative that moves me and motivates me."

"How would you describe it?" I ask. "What is the narrative?"

"Great sacrifice for others. There are a whole lot of 'one person giving deeply of themselves for other people' stories throughout history. And the story is even more attractive when it's a person who is being selfless and is fighting against what they perceive to be wrong or evil or unjust."

It's an interesting way of sounding for one's own motivation: listening for which cultural stories, which myths and legends, are most compelling. As Elliot continues to explore this idea, he summarizes another popular tale that he recognizes as having resonance for many people: the one about a person who starts out with nothing and builds or creates something significant.

"While that's a perfectly good story, it's not one that appeals to me or motivates me in the same way," Elliot says in a manner that makes me suspect this is something he has known about himself for a while. "I mean, there are probably some people who see themselves very much as motivated by the story of, I had nothing, and I'm a self-made person; I built this up. I can see someone building a law firm or a political structure or anything based on that. But that's not what motivates me. The story that motivates me or that appeals to me viscerally is the person who is at some sort of power disadvantage struggling and sacrificing to bring about some greater good."

"Where is the defense attorney in that?"

"Well, we all cast ourselves as the hero, right? So in that story we are the person who is giving. We are the one sacrificing for the greater good."

Elliot laughs at little at casting himself as the hero, but for me the heart of his metaphor isn't about how heroic he or other capital defenders may come across. The essence of it is in his saying, "This is the story that moves me." This is the gut-level pull, the thing that speaks to him in the most fundamental way.

Those early internships, like the "clinics" in which law students get to work on real cases, also offer exposure to experienced attorneys who can serve as inspiration. "They were phenomenally dedicated, talented people," recalls Nick of the attorneys he met through his own internship. Benjamin describes the first capital defenders he met as "this group of lawyers that you thought, I would give anything to be like these people: dynamic, smart, really committed. That's what I aspired to get to be part of." Julian remembers one morning in constitutional law class when the ordinarily quiet and contained professor "came bounding down the stairs and up to the podium, energized, and went into a 15-minute very excited description of what had just happened in [a particular case], how he had been up all night with other lawyers trying to get a stay [of execution]. This was the most excitement and genuine engagement that I had seen in a professor during my first year of law school." Julian signed up for his school's capital punishment clinic. There's a sense in many of these early stories of young people finding the colleagues who strike them as their people, those with whom they identify.

There's also a sense of catching the fever. Gina says it outright when she explains that after participating in her school's capital punishment clinic, she was "really hooked." *Hooked on what, exactly?* one might ask. Part of it may be the way in which capital defense satisfies the various desires I have described: to be challenged intellectually, to meet a need, to sacrifice for others, to respond rather than pass by. But another central aspect of capital defense is the intensity that its high stakes engenders. "It's like playing in the World Series all the time," explains Isabel. "You sort of start to become an adrenaline junkie after a while."

That phrase "adrenaline junkie" came up enough times in the interviews that I understood it as one the attorneys use jokingly or speculatively among themselves, lightly mocking their own motives or, more seriously, trying to understand them. Pamela uses it when she talks about her early days of work at a capital defense office.

> The second day I went down to see a guy who had three days left on his warrant . . . and I remember walking in and I was just about to throw up because, oh my God, this is really what I'm doing. You know, you can read about it, but—I just started reeling. It was overwhelming. But immediately, I jumped into the fire, which was great. I mean, we're all adrenaline junkies, no question. I think anybody who does this work, you have to be.

Rather than running for the hills at her first encounter with this overwhelming intensity, Pamela, like others who stay with this work, was ultimately more galvanized than drained by it. To do any kind of life-at-stake work, one has to be able to tolerate high levels of stress and urgency. But the attorneys' use of the word "junkie" suggests that they recognize something in themselves that doesn't just tolerate urgency but actually craves it.

My guess is that it's a fine line, for anyone, between tolerating or even thriving under certain conditions and actively *needing* those conditions in order to feel fulfilled. Obviously, the word "junkie" carries a negative connotation and suggests the possibility that people who choose this kind of work are meeting some need within themselves while they are ostensibly working on behalf of others.

Maybe they are. It's not hard to imagine that these capital defenders are indeed satisfying something within themselves through their work, but perhaps not any more so than someone in another vocation. Any freely chosen activity that a person sticks with for a long time must be personally gratifying on some level; it would be unrealistic to assume otherwise. But when that activity can so obviously be justified in terms of someone else's need, personal justification may seem unnecessary. Individuals facing execution desperately need legal representation. If they want to, attorneys can explain their choice on the basis of that need and avoid looking deeper for a personal motivation.

In addition, it sometimes seems as if questions about personal gratification are raised in an attempt to uncover the "real" motivation behind a false front of altruism—as though one type of motivation were more authentic than another. But what if both are real: the pull toward an urgent, external need and the personal gratification that comes from responding to it?

Reflecting not only on why she entered the capital defense world but, especially, on why she stays in it, Karen says, "I think it's extraordinary work that needs to be done"—a succinct summary of the motivations I've enumerated here. Karen continues, "It's got to be a type that does this work, and I don't know if we're adrenaline junkies or all have some kind of savior complex or what the deal is." When I ask her to list the possible attributes of a capital defender personality type, Karen says wryly, "None of it is good!"

What makes motivation bad or good? Karen is fairly self-mocking here, but there's a kernel of actual self-examination underlying these wry comments from Karen and her colleagues. How pure does one's motivation have to be, and are some motivations harder to admit?

Looking back on his first experience with capital defense as a summer intern, Tim acknowledges that part of the draw for him, as a young man, was the idea of some day working a high-profile case. He could picture the attention he would get and how others might respond to him.

At first glance, it would seem that capital defense is not the vocation to choose if you're looking for accolades. When large segments of the public either support the death penalty or wonder why a lawyer would devote so much energy to defending "monsters," capital defense doesn't seem like a logical choice for someone whose sense of self worth rests heavily on others' approval. But in another way, it's possible to find righteous pleasure in doing something that is not widely praised but that carries a kind of beleaguered moral authority. Moreover, it's possible to feel a private smugness about being able to tolerate what others would or could not.

"There are a lot of opportunities to *feel* righteous in this work," Tim says. It's partly the sense not only of siding with the underdog but of actually *being* the underdog. You can say, as Tim puts it, "The government is coming with all these resources, and we're so outmanned." One can hope for and imagine receiving attention for exactly that—working so hard with so little. Tim explains further, "It's not something anybody would ever say out loud, and even to yourself, I mean I never said it to myself at the time, but it's clearly an aspect of this: the idea that these are high-profile cases, and you'll get a lot of attention. . . . You don't want to say, because it's embarrassing, that it's about your lack of self-esteem and the attention you want."

From Tim's tone, I can tell that this is something he did a lot of thinking about after his internship the summer before his final year of law school. He says that eventually, after some hard-hitting self-examination,

"[I] realized I didn't need to be a death penalty lawyer to get attention. But I could see that when I wasn't self-aware, that was a driving motivation in doing the work. That what would sneak in subconsciously was, this is the sort of work that people will say, Wow, isn't that interesting—tell me about it. And you'll get attention for it."

Tim says this easily enough now, but he remembers that he was embarrassed when he initially came to the realization all those years ago. It led him to question whether he still wanted to pursue capital defense. "Is there still value to it?" he asked himself. "Is it still interesting enough, is it worthwhile, will it be fulfilling?"

Tim considered his own questions so seriously that he took a break from capital defense and worked, successfully, in other areas of law. But after a while he realized he wasn't happy. As he explains, "I saw that what I was doing was not very fulfilling. It just wasn't satisfying, doing what I was doing then. I thought, you know, I'd rather make half the money and do [capital] defense. It's much more interesting to me, and there's really a need for it, so I'll do it."

Having looked squarely at those aspects of his motivation that had been less conscious and harder to accept, Tim eventually came back to all the other reasons he found death penalty work so compelling, and he found in those reasons a way to return to the work and to feel good about doing it. Did he eradicate, through this personal inventory, the desire for attention that he had originally noticed in himself? It sounds as if in part he did. When he says, "I realized I didn't need to be a death penalty lawyer to get attention," he suggests that he reached a point where he could thrive in rather than depend upon the conditions of his work. But is the desire for attention entirely gone? Who's to say? Does it even need to be? Again I come back to the question, what makes a motivation good or bad, and how pure does motivation have to be?

Tim's reflections suggest that one way to evaluate motivation is to ask if, by choosing particular work, one is looking for something that it is unrealistic or even unhealthy to expect the work to provide. Another way is to ask whether a particular motivation negatively affects a person's ability to do the work or the way in which he or she does it. If the answer to both these questions leans toward no, then maybe it's possible to accept that a range of motivations inevitably fuels any undertaking.

Whatever their mix of motivations, the attorneys I interviewed were quite aware of the kind of attorney they *don't* want to be. As they define it, that means not giving one's best, trying to get away with the minimum, and not taking seriously the fact that a life is at stake.

Talking about his tendency to work extremely long hours at the end of a case, Gabe says, "Part of what drove me into the work in the first place is defense lawyers doing bad work. And I don't want to be one of those lawyers." There can be many reasons to want to avoid being that kind of lawyer. I suspect that, in addition to considerations of outcome and public record, one's personal sense of identity is also an issue. Gabe doesn't say, "I don't want to be *seen as* one of those lawyers." He says he doesn't want to *be* one of those lawyers, and my guess is it's as much about what he would face in the mirror as it is about what others might say about him.

At the post-conviction stage, a capital defender inherits a case that other attorneys have worked on earlier. Much of post-conviction work involves looking back at the client's previous legal record and finding errors or omissions. Tim recalls his first exposure to this.

> We weren't picking apart little legal niceties, you know, what
> the public thinks, procedural errors. I mean, these trials were
> extremely unfair. I thought, getting into the work, we'd do these
> habeas cases and the [trial] lawyers would've done a good job and
> we'd be trying to find some legal issue to make hay out of. What
> I found was surprising, that the trial lawyers were terrible—of the
> cases that we had. Certainly there were a lot of good ones, but most
> of those good ones, their clients probably weren't on death row. But
> the clients that ended up on death row, man, the lawyers were just
> shockingly terrible.

This is a key point, albeit a volatile one. These post-conviction lawyers aren't saying all trial lawyers are bad at what they do (and some of the attorneys I interviewed had previously worked or still do work at both the trial and post-conviction stages). But almost by definition (at least from the defense's perspective) the death penalty cases that reach a post-conviction attorney's desk are those for which the lawyering at the trial level was at best inadequate and at worst egregiously bad—otherwise, the trial would not have resulted in a death sentence. While this may not be true across the board, it's a generalization these attorneys feel they have cause to make. "I don't get the cases where people had really good lawyers at the trial stage," is the way several explained it to me. Inheriting cases for which the lawyers had manifestly *not* done everything they could, these attorneys now have a stark comparison against which to measure themselves. They know that an attorney coming in at the post-conviction stage has to be very different from the "shockingly terrible" trial attorney to have even the slimmest chance of overcoming the death sentence—and of overcoming the client's feeling that lawyers are people who let you down.

One variation on the "I can't help but fight it" idea represented by Julian's comments at the beginning of this chapter is the statement "I can't live with myself if I don't." With this feeling as their guideline, these attorneys often see only one viable approach even when they technically have a choice about how to do their work. Should they give every ounce of effort? Should they get to know their clients as individuals? If they consider whether they would be able to live with themselves afterward, the answers become inevitable. They are motivated not just to do this work but do it in certain ways—which in turn reinforces their individual and collective identities.

"I think in the death penalty community that I come from," says Benjamin, "we do things that have no chance of succeeding because we have a collective norm about what constitutes meaningful representation." He offers this as an explanation for why he might take an action—like filing a last-ditch, long-shot clemency petition—that he knows has little chance of being effective.

> I do that in part because I don't want to be like the lawyers who *don't* do that, the lawyers who don't appear to care about their

clients. It's talismanic to me: it may have no chance of succeeding, but by doing this, I lay down the marker that I am a different kind of lawyer than those people. You know, I am part of the people I aspire to be like—I'm with them. I'm doing this as a way of signing that I am part of that group.

Benjamin may not be able to control the outcome of the case, but he can decide, and signify to others, the kind of lawyer he wants to be. This, as much as (or maybe more than) anything else, constitutes his motivation.

The first lecture Isabel heard on the subject of the death penalty was in a class during her first year of law school. She found it enthralling. When I ask what enthralled her, she first cites what are by now familiar motivations: the legal issues were fascinating, the human story compelling. She then elaborates, "To me, doing death penalty work has always been about what it's supposed to be about to be a lawyer, which I think a lot of lawyers lose track of, that you really are supposed to help people. You know, it's the *To Kill a Mockingbird* philosophy: if you're a lawyer, you need to have at least one case that changes you. Well, if you're a death penalty lawyer, *all* your cases change you in some way."

Drawn to capital defense for a variety of reasons both emotional and intellectual, these attorneys practice high-stakes law in ways that align with some of the deepest parts of themselves. If they initially came to the work with a desire to change something, I'm guessing it wasn't themselves. But as Isabel suggests, doing the work in the way that they are driven to do it inevitably leaves them open to being affected by all that they encounter. The "I" that could not help but take up this fight also cannot help but be changed by its crucible of demand and reward.

# CHAPTER 3

# The Responsibility

"TO WHAT EXTENT does it feel like, 'It's on me to stop this execution'?"

Pamela answers immediately, "Oh, yeah. It *is*." It's a telling choice of words: not it *does* feel that way, but oh yes, it *is* that way.

"I think you have to feel that," Pamela continues. "You have to think that with every client, it's on you. If I don't feel like it's on me, then there's nothing I can do, and then I don't. You know, I'm always looking for a way out! So I have to feel like, This is my game, this is my story, this is my problem."

I ask if she felt that early on, with her first capital case, and she says she did, if only because when she first started practicing capital defense, there were so many execution warrants that "you were immediately assigned a case and told to get to work." There was no one else to whom you could shift the responsibility even if you wanted to. But even now, a couple of decades later, Pamela says that she doesn't fundamentally want to shift the responsibility. That sense of "it's on me" keeps her motivated, "keeps the fire going."

I ask, "Is there a down side to thinking 'it's on me'?"

"Oh, of course. It's not healthy, is it? But I guess part of where that comes from is listening to the jurors, listening to the judges—'It's nobody's fault.' You know, it goes back to the concentration camps and the idea that nobody's in charge, nobody takes responsibility."

Earlier in our interview, Pamela talked about having been drawn since childhood to literature about the Holocaust and other writing describing the horrors of war. She makes the connection for herself as she speaks:

"I think that's probably—I've *never* thought about this before, but that's probably where this feeling comes from, because that's where I started in this whole, you know, thinking about the horrors of the world. 'It's nobody's fault.' It *has* to be somebody's fault. It has to be my fault, it has to be your fault—"

"Meaning, you want to step up in some way?"

"Yes. It *is* my fault. That doesn't make it nobody else's fault, but I've got to take personal responsibility for it."

"What's the 'it' in that?"

"For what we're doing as a society. For allowing this man to die. For allowing this to continue, for allowing this horror to continue, on all these levels."

Pamela's insistence on claiming her share of the societal "fault" for the death penalty echoes Eric's comment about having a "social responsibility" to defend clients on death row. Eric cited that feeling as motivation for getting into death penalty work in the first place. In Pamela's comments we begin to see the distinct shape that responsibility assumes once a capital defender is actually representing a client who has been sentenced to death and is facing execution. The question is no longer only, "To what extent do I, as a citizen, feel a share of responsibility for what my society does?" Agreeing to represent a client in a capital case means not only feeling but also very explicitly *accepting* a distinct kind of responsibility toward a particular human being. The urgency (a life is at stake) and the personal specificity (*I* am the one who has signed up for this task) come together into something both galvanizing and terrifying. It might keep the fire going, but it can also keep you up at night.

Because Pamela was immediately handed a case at the death warrant stage, and because she was surrounded by other attorneys who had already lost clients, the possibility of an execution felt very real to her almost as soon as she started work. But in the early stretch of the modern death penalty era, most attorneys had not yet personally experienced the loss of a client to execution, nor did they have close colleagues who had experienced that loss. Paul recalls,

> When I started, people weren't being executed. As time passed, it got more and more real, and within five years I'd had four clients executed, so it got real pretty quickly. But [initially] it was unthinkable to me that any of my clients would be executed. Until they were. I wasn't prepared for it. I'm not sure how I could've been, but I certainly wasn't.

> *What took you by surprise?*

> How, with an execution date set, how that sort of changed everything in your life towards a riveting focus on this person's case, that you thought you'd given all your attention to before, but you move to another level of thinking about the case, thinking about what other things you might do, higher levels of energy, just total focus.

In a way, though, no one can really prepare, no matter how real the prospect seems when one first gets involved with a case. Recalling how it felt to take on his first capital case, well after the resumption of executions in the United States and with plenty of examples and others' experiences available, Elliot says, "The execution itself was still abstract. It was very much I could define myself as being against the forces of death, against forces of darkness, in a melodramatic way, but I didn't know what it was like."

Maybe what one knows at the outset is simply, or primarily, the feeling of urgency and the demand for intense focus that Paul described. This is so clearly not the run-of-the-mill legal work that these attorneys rejected when they were considering what to do with a law license. They'd wanted the feeling of helping where help was most needed, engaging in work of obvious significance, and then they got it—so much so that the words they use to describe the undertaking are often less legal than moral, interpersonal, even existential. Nick describes an early case he helped with as a second-year law student.

> That's the first case that I felt, "That's mine."
>
> *What was it like to feel that?*
>
> It was exhilarating, it was scary. . . .
>
> *What was the exhilarating part?*
>
> Just to feel that I was part of trying to save somebody's life.

As Nick begins to suggest, the feeling of working to save a life, and even a feeling of ownership for that effort, doesn't necessarily correlate with the actual degree of responsibility that one has for a case. Regardless of their precise roles, attorneys may feel that particular cases belong to them because of—for example—how much of their own lives they spend working on the case, or the level of investment they feel in the outcome, or the amount of time they've spent with the client, or how devastated they later are by the loss.

True, there are times when one might be literally the only person working on a case. Julian remembers how "horrifying" it was to realize that "nobody else was going to step in for this guy" in a crisis situation in which the two court-appointed attorneys weren't doing any work on the case. Julian, who like Nick was not even officially a lawyer at that point, spent his own money on the investigation and stayed up for several nights writing the legal petition. As Julian says of that client, "He was defenseless without me," a phrase I find evocative for both its legal and personal meaning.

Though the investment in a case can be considerable regardless of the technical description of the attorney's role, there is a significant difference between simply being "a part of trying to save somebody's life" and being solely responsible for making key strategic decisions in the effort to save a life. "You ask, how were you *feeling?*" Keith repeats back to me with a laugh. "The whole world was upside down! There was a lot more anxiety than I'm used to feeling or admitting—ever."

Roger describes feeling more acutely affected by the executions of clients he had been representing for several years—in comparison to some of his early cases where he had known the clients for much less time—and then goes on to say,

> And the other part of it is, those were mine. Not only had I been on the cases for that long, but I'd been making the calls and running the show.

*Does that make it feel different?*

> You know, it *does* feel different, both in terms of—I think of some of the early cases where [someone else was] the lead counsel; he's making all the decisions, and I was just doing stuff. I'm writing the pleadings, but he's deciding the strategies. So it is different. When you're sitting there going, I'm now the one making those decisions. There's nobody else I can fall back on. I mean, I've got other folks around me, but ultimately, it falls on me—that is a different feeling. It's an increased burden of responsibility.

Gabe, too, distinguishes between simply helping out on a case and knowing that "the buck stops with you," but he also acknowledges that even when one doesn't have the final responsibility, the pressure can still be considerable.

> [Working in teams] I think is critical for young lawyers to come in and have people that you felt confident in, someone you could look up to and say, I trust this person's judgment. So you didn't necessarily feel like—the buck didn't stop with you. Yet, at the same time, being sent out to do something and knowing that if you succeed, it will really help the case, and if you *can't* pull off whatever it is you're going to do—there's that pressure. So I think you always have a sense of ownership, I guess—that's a weird word for it, but a sense of responsibility to the case. But a case where the buck *did* stop with me didn't come until a couple of years later.

[With that one,] I had more experienced people to talk to about the case, but I still felt like it was on my shoulders. . . . I tried very, very hard to stop that execution. I felt like it was all on me to stop it. It's a tremendous weight.

Having others to consult with is critical when you're starting out and the buck *doesn't* yet stop with you; it's also a vital part of the work even when you know the final responsibility is yours. Several attorneys echoed the following comment from Caroline about capital defenders nationwide:

It is a tremendous group of people. I mean, they are—you almost don't have to ask for help because they're there. So it does give you a tremendous feeling of being supported. The lawyers who do [this work] are a phone call away, and nobody ever says no. It's a reassuring feeling because you're making life and death decisions and to have people either sort of guide you in a different direction or just reassure you that what you're doing is OK, or you can call them if you're not sure.

And this from Nick:

What makes it easier for me is that I have that group of people I can call on who I really respect and think the world of. . . . I go to these people and say, this is the situation, and [we] talk it through. So I have that, I believe it's a safety net, a security blanket: I've talked to them, they're a lot smarter than me, they believe this is the way to go. So I'm OK.

But even working as part of a defense team or having trusted colleagues at the ready doesn't necessarily liberate an attorney from an intensely personal struggle with the demands of trying to stop an execution. An individual's involvement in a capital case ultimately demands an individual reckoning, regardless of the attorney's precise role on the team. Capital defense is often characterized by a precious and keenly felt solidarity with others who do the work, a sense of being together in a crucible that few outside can fully understand. At the same time, there's a way in which—emotionally and sometimes also practically—each attorney is also alone with the responsibility, the fear, the self-doubt, and, sometimes, the grief.

There are a few safety nets—or, as some attorneys put it, "shelters"—that can buffer an attorney from the harshness of absolute responsibility for saving a life. Because overturning a death sentence is usually assumed to be more difficult than preventing a death sentence from being handed down in the first place, attorneys at the post-conviction stage know that the odds are against them. As Karen puts it, "We have the shelter of getting the case when you already have ninety-nine strikes against you . . . the system is so stacked against you that anything but an execution is a miraculous outcome."

Karen describes having conversations with attorneys who work in areas—including capital defense at the trial level—where losing is less common and thus more remarkable. She laughs wryly as she describes her own reaction during these conversations, "They talk about losing and I'm like, I lose all the time! It's the norm to lose!" Losing all the time is emotionally challenging in ways that I'll soon explore further, but it's notable here that when it comes to the question of one's own responsibility for preventing the execution, the long odds can actually serve a positive function.

Somewhat ironically, another shelter can be the daily pressure of the work itself. All the tasks that need to be done are so demanding in themselves that they can make it hard to focus on anything but the immediate. Or to put it another way, they can make it easier to avoid focusing on the looming threat. The urgency of a pending execution engenders the motivation to work almost non-stop, but then the busyness can also create a buffer for the worst of the fear. Says Nick, "The thing about a warrant period is, you're working so much that you don't have time to stop and think about how scary it is." Elliot puts it this way: "There's a short-term focus that it's easy to lose yourself in, and maybe it's good to lose yourself in at some level."

Roger suggests that the short-term focus is useful not only for one's own emotional survival but also for effective work on the case.

> You can get focused on everything that's going on every day: you have to meet this deadline, have to do this investigation. So the enormity of the whole thing gets kept in check, because you'd be paralyzed otherwise. I think if all you're focused on is, "this guy's going to die if I don't do something," you just spin wheels, as opposed to jumping in and taking baby steps, doing the little steps that ultimately lead to the big picture.

So often in our interviews the attorneys would evaluate the utility of a given strategy—including an internal, emotional one—in terms of whether that strategy made it more or less possible to continue engaging in effective work. Here, the challenge is how to feel enough of a responsibility to fuel the fire that keeps you doing what's necessary, without letting the enormity of it weigh you down so heavily that you end up stuck and not doing anything at all. Like so many such things, that optimal midpoint is easy to describe but often fiercely difficult to maintain. It's not something to figure out once and then effortlessly achieve thereafter; it's a continual and probably always imperfect dance.

Whatever offsets it, there's still no question that the responsibility of trying to prevent an execution is, as Gabe puts it, a tremendous weight. After listening to Roger's description of the added responsibility that comes with being lead counsel, I ask him, "What does that added responsibility feel like? How do you carry it around?" He laughs and says, "In my shoulders! In the muscles in my neck!" The burden is not just metaphoric but actual, physical. Says Lou of this same feeling,

> His life is on my shoulders. It's terribly stressful and burdensome. It is personally, for me, almost unbearable. I've had to develop some defenses, not to dream about cases. I try to manage my life so I don't

have too many cases. . . . I can't live with myself unless I feel like it's a number I can manage.

Benjamin describes it this way:

> I really do carry [the responsibility] around. All of us carry it around, all the time. We're worried we're going to fuck something up, and someone's going to die as a result of that. Or, worse, that we'll to do the best we can, and they'll die anyway.

And Nick:

> It's got to be your number one priority, because it's somebody else's life in your hands. It's a privilege. And that's why you can't—that's why you need to be better than other people. Well, no, not "I'm a better person," but you have to work harder. You can't afford—well, *you* can, but your clients can't afford for you not to know everything.

As we'll see in the next chapter, Nick suffers mightily from the loss of his clients, but he seems to accept with relative equanimity the demands of trying to save them. It's what the work is, and he's accepted this as his work. It was a tone that characterized many of his responses to my questions. Still, it's interesting to contemplate what's inherent in the statement "your clients can't afford for you not to know everything." This is why the attorneys talk about not sleeping for several nights running, or why it can feel as if any other demand on their time, anything that seems less urgent, is a distraction from the matter at hand.

Sometimes, the sheer number of tasks is so overwhelming as to seem impossible. Those who talked about working at the federally funded capital resource centers during the 1990s, for example, or at other offices or agencies at times when the execution dates were coming fast and furious, made me think of doctors in war-time MASH units or any other environment where there is too much coming in at once, all of it urgent, and the responders not only have to attempt triage but also have to essentially ignore their own needs for rest or replenishment. Gabe remembers, "We'd stay up all night for a week working on a case, then the guy was executed, then we would come in again and do it again, week after week." I ask how they sustained that, and he shakes his head ruefully: "I don't know."

Gina talks about the stress that comes from knowing that "the amount of work is not humanly possible to do within the time frame."

> Realistically I know that it's not all on me, because I know it depends on who the judge is or the other team members or how meritorious the claims are or whatever—I know that intellectually, but the feeling I have is, You'd better put your best effort, or your client will be executed.

> *What's it like to carry that?*

> It's gotten easier in a way; I've learned how to handle it. The first years were harder, I think. Non-stop stress. All the time having this sense of impending doom. Now I think I've learned how to manage it better.

> *How would you say you've learned to handle it or mange it?*

> It has changed in the sense that I don't feel it all the time, but I feel it when I have a deadline or when we have a hearing or other big events like that, that sort of feeling comes back, but day to day I tell myself, You're doing the best you can; just work steadily.

I heard this frequently: an attorney's assessment of having gotten better at handling the stress was based on something like "not being consumed by it every minute." The level of pressure they'd come to accept as ordinary was often quite remarkable to me.

About halfway through our interview, Paul muses about the idea of not doing capital defense work—almost as a hypothetical exercise in imagining what it might be like to live a completely different kind of life: "I can *imagine* what it would be like not to wake up early feeling stress immediately upon gaining enough consciousness to know that it's morning—"

He trails off. I wait a moment. I'm sure my incredulity is apparent as I ask, "You feel that every day?"

He nods, laughing a little as he realizes how it sounds. "I could imagine what it would be like to wake up in the morning and feel unstressed, but I don't *know* what it's like."

We continue talking about other things for a while and then, about ten minutes later, Paul, like Gina above, observes that the pressure has gotten easier to manage over the years. "I don't feel the acute stress the way that I did [in the early days]," he explains.

"Waking up every morning feeling it?" It's hard not to recall the remark he has just made.

"That's true. That's true, but that's normal!" This time he throws back his head and laughs heartily, in the way that people do when they see something about themselves that someone else's inquiry has made visible. Then he becomes quiet, reflective. I ask how he would characterize "acute stress," the kind he says he feels less of these days.

"Acute stress is paralyzing, feeling like you're going to come out of your skin, feeling like you're losing it, or screaming, or just—it's breakdown sort of stress." He pauses to think further. "That happens when you've got a number of things to get done and you can't get them all done in the same period of time. It's that kind of thing. That happens relatively often—you know, probably not more than once a week, but it can happen once a week."

He laughs again as he says "once a week," no doubt sensing that a part of me is thinking *that still sounds like quite a lot.*

He continues, "So I guess what's happened over time with me is I have less acute stress, or these peaks of stress. Stress is more spread out, and my acute periods have to do more with having five things that I need to do in this space where I can only do one of them, and just being near the point of breakdown trying to figure out how to do anything."

"Because they're all equally important?"

"Well, irrationally they are. [Eventually you] try to sort of calm down, think about it, and develop a plan. Because you can always do that. But in the midst of these feelings, you can't. They're all utterly un-doable and utterly imperative."

Subjectively, Paul truly does feel that something about the stress has gotten easier to manage, and I don't doubt him. Yet for the listener, it's hard not to be left astonished at the degree of pressure and urgency that may sound untenable but is, apparently, possible to become acclimated to.

Even when the actual workload is manageable—however one might define that—there's also an untenable feeling that comes not from the number of tasks but from the sense that anything else one does is somehow less essential. Says Karen,

> When a client gets an execution date, it's like the big dark cloud for many weeks or months. It's a really hard thing to live with, the rising panic. . . . It's always present. It's hard to live your life, it's hard to go grocery shopping, take your child out to play baseball, do the stuff that is your life—that goes on while you do this year after year.

*When is it hardest?*

> When an execution date is looming, you can feel like, what am I doing going to the park with my child? You know, Aaaah! Somebody's life is in your hands. How can you do anything else?

It's a tension so vividly drawn that I feel as if I'm experiencing it for a moment as I listen to Karen. How can you do anything else? But how can you not? As several others also said, those other things, including the ordinary demands and pleasures of family life, are also the counterweight that makes the work possible or at least endurable. And those ordinary demands, particularly of parenthood, are in their own way as non-negotiable—which, Karen observed, can actually help (or force) a capital defender to set limits on the work and maintain some kind of balance.

But still, the tensions persist. The continual urgent pull of the work affects not only the time the attorneys can spend with their families but also the quality of that time. Paul recalls a particularly intense period when his children were young.

> I struggled with trying to be present for my children. I would get up at 4:00 in the morning and work for two to three hours before they got up so I could be with them before they went to school, and then I'd get home at an hour that I could be with them in the evenings, and then if I had to work the rest of the night, I'd work the rest of the night.
>
> *Did it ever feel the other way, like I'm not doing enough for this case because I'm with the family?*
>
> Not generally, because I would just not sleep. Because I couldn't live with that feeling.

Similarly, Pamela says,

> I know that if I could have the luxury—if I could work 24/7 and devote myself to this one case, then I could do it better and not feel pulled in two directions. But I can't work all the time, so the pressure is always there. And that's why I grind my teeth.

And Simon describes it this way:

> Most of the news we get in our cases is bad news, it's a development . . . the court wants to move something along, a brief has been filed by the other side that says things you wish they'd forgotten or didn't see, you've got a deadline that you didn't have five minutes ago. Shit, what am I going to do now? And I do know that these negative interventions can really kind of throw me off. I know that I'll be in the middle of something [with the family], whatever, and I'll get something, and I'm sure, you know, my tone changes; I'm less present.

Though there were other aspects of the way capital defense work has affected him that it seemed Simon was only just realizing or articulating during the course of our interview, this feeling of not always being fully present while with the family was one he was already quite aware of. That struck me as true with the others who described this feeling too. Roger remembered talking with his daughter about a case just as he was about to enter the intense period of working under a death warrant. He was trying to tell her that he had this one reasonably under control; the intensity would last for a finite period, and then it would be over.

> She said, "Well, that may be so, but we all know that when you have an execution warrant you're not present even when you're with us."

*How did you take that?*

> I just sort of chuckled to myself and thought, all right, that's right. Because, you know, how do you go from work where you're dealing with real, literal, life-and-death questions and issues and come home and just—click, it's off? . . . She didn't say anything I didn't know, but it was interesting that she had that perception. You know, I had to say, OK, you're right, but this is going to be over in a few weeks, and hopefully I'll be back.

Roger goes on to talk about how, with any intense writing job, he's always working subconsciously even if he's not actually at his desk. The ideas are "spinning and processing in the background," as he puts it. Roger finds that to be true even when he's working on material for other types of cases.

"You're describing a familiar aspect of the creative process in general," I say, "and then it seems like this death penalty stuff must have an extra dose of—"

"Terror," Roger says, finishing my sentence. We've been talking about the creative process and suddenly we are here, at this stark description of the fear that accompanies capital defense work.

"So terror, however foreground or background, could certainly make a person less present."

"Right."

Roger brings up another consequence of the responsibility inherent in capital defense work: a very particular kind of arrogance. There can be a tendency, he says, to think, "We are the saviors, the heart surgeons, pulling people back from the dead, and everything we do is the most important thing out there because our clients are going to die." This self-perception can affect the way capital defenders interact with each other.

> It becomes—I mean, it's a good motivational tool, to realize how important [the work] is, but it also leads to fights about petty things, or if there's disagreement about a strategic issue, "Oh, we can't do it your way because you're going to kill the client."

> *It becomes a kind of trump?*

> Exactly.

Roger tells stories of the wry joking that this kind of fighting can lead to, but inside the humor his comments acknowledge a complexity: a life *is* at stake, and a misguided legal strategy will put that life at even greater risk. At the same time, attorneys' awareness of that fact, and even precisely their skill and expertise in evaluating or carrying out the legal strategies, can engender the kind of grandiosity that Roger describes. As we discuss this further, I return to the original question of whether it's the capital defender's responsibility to try to save the client's life. Roger's response sums up the subtle but crucial distinction he himself has come to.

> Well, I believe that. We all believe that. It *is* our responsibility. But I think it's one thing to have that as your sort of driving principle as opposed to having that as your—well, I think it's the difference between having it as your identity and having it as your goal. It's

hard to articulate, but in one sense it's almost an egotistical thing: "I am the person on the front lines," you know. There's a personal investment in that, in your identity; your identity *is* the savior, as opposed to realizing that it's what you have to do—it's what you're trying very hard to do—but it's not who you are.

As wise as I find Roger's distinction, I can imagine how some attorneys could experience the challenge of trying to save another human being so viscerally that the effort could start to feel inextricable from their identity—who they are, not just what they do. I think of Nick's saying that capital defense isn't just a job; it's a way of life—though he also describes his family's agreement not to talk about work at the dinner table. This is probably another one of those continual tensions that can never be resolved once and for all. Everyone has to sort it out in some way, or try to, and some of the attorneys spoke explicitly about their need to draw lines or keep some parts of their lives separate.

Roger brings up the "savior complex" in terms of how it can affect interactions among colleagues; Simon talks about how the same phenomenon can cause friction within a marriage or a family.

> I was late for something . . . and it was a tense moment in the car and [my wife] was basically expressing frustration with me being late because of work. I said in all seriousness, but it's become a joke that I even said it, I said something like, "I'm sorry that I was late— I was just saving lives!" And I was real serious and offended that she would not appreciate the need for me to do my work because it was so all-important. Now it's a joke; it's a thing we say that's sort of funny.

Obviously, people who are already prone to seeing themselves as more important than others, or who are looking for an excuse not to meet the needs or fulfill the requests of the other people in their lives, could take cover under the excuse of high-pressure, high-demand work. But when I think of these stories in the context of all the other reflections on what it's like to engage in capital defense work, I can't help wondering if this arrogance, when it does surface in these attorneys or others they describe, might not be at least partly a defense against a sometimes intolerable burden of responsibility, or the fear that underlies it.

That fear—the terror that Roger speaks of—inevitably leads attorneys to second-guess whether they've made a mistake or could have done something different, or more, or better.

> That feeling never goes away: could I have done something differently? I've had periods where I've worked all night every night for three nights in a row . . . you know, go seventy-two hours on four hours of sleep or something like that. The adrenaline that kicks in at times is, for me, I think, driven by, "I have to do everything I can possibly think of." Because I don't want to walk away from something thinking, "If I had just done. . . ." It feels like, the weight of it, and the *fear*, I think—fear of making a mistake or overlooking something or not doing something right. –Gabe

> You feel like you're the only thing between your client and him getting executed. If you feel like you're doing a good job and might get some results, it's OK, but it can definitely weigh on you, especially if you think you might have made mistakes or something like that—that can keep you up at night. There was one case I was really distraught over; it was coming up for a hearing. At the time I kind of felt like I was alone working on it, and I just—I was unable to sleep. It was pretty awful. . . . I think that by and large I handle that kind of stuff pretty well, but it's just kind of the thoughts that creep into your head without any kind of—you know, what you should be doing, what you didn't do, that kind of thought will just pop in. And then I'll start feeling bad: I should've done that; why didn't I go and do this? Stuff like that makes you feel guilty, basically. That's the thing, I think: the guilt comes very easily, even if you may be doing all you can do. There's always questions, there's always second-guessing, and then there's always guilt. –Eric

It's really tough for me. I don't think I'm entirely ever going to be able to say it's not partly my fault. . . . I won't say that I often feel I should've worked harder, because I feel like I work as hard as I can. There's almost no psychological space for me to say I should've worked harder, because I know that wouldn't have been possible. But it's the worry that I should have made a different decision . . . that I didn't see early enough where this was going and have a Plan B, some other way to—well, but the answer is, there's no way out of the maze. There is no exit. But when you run into the wall, it's so easy to say, If we'd just taken a left turn back there, we'd be out of here by now. It's never true, but it's what you feel. –Benjamin

Listening to the attorneys describe these doubts and inevitable second-guessing, I have the sense that they are at least to some degree describing it for themselves, to themselves, even as they are ostensibly explaining it to me. In these comments, I see how they are thinking aloud, hitting upon the crux of it as they go: the fear of making a mistake is what keeps them going non-stop for so many days. The guilt comes easily, almost irrespective of the actual quality or thoroughness of their work.

And then that guilt and second-guessing leave a mark that distinguishes this loss from other losses in a defense attorney's life. Keith says he experiences the "hollowness" after a client's execution as recognizably different from the way he has felt after losing members of his own family.

When you lose clients, there's a sense of responsibility. You think there's something else you could've done, should've done. You think, If someone else had been the lawyer, if someone else had done this . . . *someone* should've been able to, why couldn't you, why didn't you? So, yeah, part of it is a sense of responsibility and guilt. And actually, I'm not [otherwise] a person who second-guesses. I make a decision—I'm happy with it, usually. You know, I lose cases, I can't say I'm happy about it, but I generally am able to close the book on it. Actually that's what I prided myself on before. . . . When you lose a client, none of that operates. I mean, you just sort of constantly are thinking about, What if you had done this, what if you had done that, let's do this. But you can't; it's too late.

What can talk back to these doubts? Nick offers one possibility:

> I talk to people who are coming in now and I say, There are going to be places where you could go one way or the other, and if you sit down and you reason through it, you talk through it, you look at both options, and you make a choice, and [later] it doesn't turn out to be the right choice, it's not a mistake.

That way of seeing things doesn't erase all doubt, but, Nick suggests, it can stop the endless wheel-spinning and middle-of-the-night wondering. If you thought it through carefully and had a good reason for doing what you did, then you don't have to beat yourself up about it if it turns out you weren't able to foresee everything. Nestled inside Nick's rationale is a basic recognition of human limitation—and this is from the same attorney who says, "Your client can't afford for you not to know everything." Even if you could, in some sense, know everything, you still can't predict the myriad other factors and variables outside of your own control.

Tim is particularly firm on the idea that responsibility's limits are clearly delineated.

> I view my job as very clear: doing my best, working my hardest to do what I can in the legal case to stop my client from getting executed. That's my responsibility. I'm not responsible for whether he lives or dies. . . . We're not responsible for any outcomes, because there are so many things you can't control. That's my personal view. You're not responsible for what actually happens; you're responsible for making the effort. That's a fine distinction, but I think a very important one. And it makes a difference.

I think of Thomas Merton's words "Do not depend on the hope of results." Or the Tao te Ching's "Do your work, then step back." Do what's yours, and don't take on what isn't. For those in demanding, high-stakes work, this guiding principle is both a comfort and an aspiration. Acceptance of human limitation doesn't come easily, even when humans crash up against it time and time again. It's not only that some things can't be foreseen or are outside of one's control; it's also that, inevitably, somewhere, we hit the wall of our own capacity.

"I never feel I've done everything I could," says Paul, an experienced capital defender whose capacity others often rely on. "Because I don't think of everything, or I get tired, I fall asleep—"

He smiles at this; it's such a mundane example, when set against the transcendence of fighting for someone's life. But given how often the attorneys speak of staying up all night or running for weeks on extremely little rest, "falling asleep" begins to seem like a metaphor for yielding to the needs of the body, and even for the concept of limitation itself. In the end, one is never going to be able to accomplish the vaguely imagined idea of "everything" that it might be possible to do for a case.

Paul tells of meeting a renowned capital defender years ago and hearing something that has stayed with him.

> He talked about how one of the most fundamental, if not the most fundamental, problems with the death penalty is that it was an infinite punishment administered by finite people who make mistakes and take shortcuts and screw up. And are frail, don't have enough energy, whatever. I've always sort of taken comfort in that.
>
> *You let that work for you.*
>
> Yes. Because there's no question about it. It is a punishment that doesn't deserve to be inflicted because the process for imposing it and carrying it out is done by frail people. It demands perfection, and there is none. Yeah, I take comfort in that.

But it remains a struggle. I hear the attorneys acknowledging their own limits while simultaneously saying, in effect, "but our clients can't afford for us to be finite, or frail, or tired." They repeatedly confront the paradox that what they consider necessary is also impossible.

Maybe one of the variables for anyone in this kind of situation is the extent to which human limitation is recognized and structurally accommodated. It seems to me that in at least some other professions in which we ask people to push themselves right up to the edge of their capacity (airline pilots and medical professionals, for example), we also build in safeguards, opportunities for relief. Here it strikes me that, for the most part, it is up to the defenders to acknowledge their own limitations and then invent their own safeguards—if they do at all.

I suspect, too, that the disparity in available safeguards comes at least in part from the difference between capital defense and other high-stakes endeavors. When the need for the effort and sacrifice is more readily understood and acknowledged (as, again, with medical professionals), it's easier to justify building in the necessary safeguards. Our societal relationship to capital defense is more ambivalent. Defense attorneys may be understood as necessary to a societal practice that is, in many parts of the United States, both legal and popular, but sympathy for the challenges inherent in their role does not necessarily follow. Attorneys worry, likely with some justification, that voicing their own distress or requesting safeguards or limits won't elicit much positive response.

Even if capital defenders have managed to recognize the limits to their capacity and responsibility, and even if they understand the odds are so great that, as Karen puts it, "anything but an execution is a miraculous outcome," they can still harbor feelings like those Gabe expresses: "Every time someone's executed, you feel like you've failed. Even if you know going into it that the deck is stacked against you." The idea of execution as failure, and particularly, as Gabe phrases it, one's *own* failure, came up several times, not necessarily as a definitive feeling but as an aspect of the experience that they turned over and examined as we spoke.

Roger and I are talking about what counts as success, a question I'll explore in Chapter 7. Roger immediately cites the obvious successes:

getting someone off death row, reversing the death sentence. After a while I ask, "So is execution a failure?" He says yes without hesitation, and, as if to illustrate the point, begins telling about his decision not to go to the funeral of a client who had recently been executed. The mitigation specialist who had worked the case, and who was much newer to death penalty work, assumed that Roger would want to go to the funeral.

> I was saying how I had some court date on Friday. She said, "You know, they may schedule the funeral on Friday." I said, "They may, but I'm not going to be there." And she was just shocked. I said, "Look, I'm just not going to sit there and wallow in failure."

*Ah, that's why you thought of that story just now.*

Yeah. I mean, it's like—no doubt.

*You immediately said yes when I asked if it's a failure. Whose failure is it?*

Oh God, it's everybody's failure. I mean, it's mine because I didn't pull it out. You think, it's the system, it's society, it's the whole culture.

It's not only one's own failure, then—there is obviously a broader social context here, the very one that Pamela and others spoke of earlier when they talked about feeling a share of responsibility for the circumstances that lead to the death penalty. But even as they recognize this, the attorneys' comments also return to an acknowledgment of capital defenders' very particular relationship to the event of an execution. Roger himself comes back to it as he says, "It is *the* most vivid example that we didn't win, didn't do what we needed to do. That's about as real as it gets."

Keith speaks vividly of the nature of that particular relationship. Though he was certainly emotionally affected when his colleagues' clients were executed, he felt an unmistakable difference when it happened to one of his own.

"It's just so deeply personal," he says. "I think when you've got the direct responsibility, you really do make this bond or this pact with the client that you're going to be there for him and that you've got his back and that you will defend him. And to me, part of that is I'm making a pact that you're not going to die. I'm not going to let them kill you, you know?"

*I'm not going to let them.* Is that even within an attorney's power to promise? Sitting with Keith in this moment, that objective question almost doesn't seem to matter. He's taking me inside his experience in a way that I can't go if I focus too much on the external legitimacy of this pact he's talking about. What I have to do is sit here and feel the emotional impact of the promise: what it would be like to carry it and, later, to feel that you have broken it.

Keith continues, "It's the notion that you put yourself between your client and the execution. And so when you fail, what that means is that they've walked *over* you and gotten your client in the chamber. I mean, it's just—it's a failure at a personal level that's just not replicated any other time. Every time you meet with the client, the unstated promise is, It ain't gonna happen. I'm not going to let it happen."

I ask him about the word *failure*, since he's used it a couple of times. Is he saying an execution is a failure? He nods but then gets quiet.

"Failure seems almost too—I mean, it seems to suggest a competitive aspect that I don't think is at the core of it," he says slowly. "It's the failure that's created by, you know, a breach of trust. You're in this deal with the client. His responsibility is to trust you, to share, to tell, to open up. You're asking the client to give, give, give, and to be patient, and he's going to have expectations, and all through the relationship you're managing those expectations, and the sort of undertone to all that is, You do all that, and [in return] I will stop them from doing this."

After another moment he adds, "For the most part, with all my post-conviction clients, they all met their part of the bargain. They did whatever I asked them to."

He stops and looks at me. I understand the next part of the thought without his having to spell it out.

"And you didn't hold up your end? You didn't keep them from being executed?"

He nods: *that's right*. And again, although part of me wants to argue for the impossibility of this pact, the limits to his responsibility, I keep silent.

Within this emotional territory, there is no *one* way that a capital defender feels. Roger speaks eloquently about not wrapping one's identity in the outcome of the case, and yet he also vividly describes his reluctance to wallow in the feeling of failure that a client's execution unavoidably presents. The emotional experience exists in layers, and there's more than one feeling to know. I think of Adam's story about the rescuer who wasn't able to save the boy after he had wandered off the hiking trail. Would Adam have said, before his unexpected reaction to that news story, that he blamed himself for not being able to prevent his clients' executions? The news story gave him access to a feeling he had been carrying and that he hadn't even fully realized was inside him until that moment.

In the exchange that opens this chapter, in which Pamela insists on seeing the death penalty as partly her fault, she speaks of a determination to claim a share of societal responsibility and to do what, in her eyes, that share demands. This kind of claim—of active citizenry but maybe also of something more specific and personal ("this is the kind of person I want to be or the way I want to live in the world")—is one way to view the concept of "fault." Something is happening, and I am partly responsible for its happening. But what about the rescuer who failed to find the lost boy in time to save him? Or a doctor whose patient dies? It can be difficult to sort out what is and is not within one's capacity, or what it means to throw oneself into a fight that is often so hard to win.

When Simon first encountered death penalty law, it seemed to him like "a labyrinth of procedural rules that if you misstep at any point [it] means death."

"What's it like to realize that?" I ask. "To behold the idea that there are a lot of missteps I could make, and if I make them, it's somebody's life?"

"I never—you know, it's funny. Probably out of absolutely undeserved hubris, I never let myself blame myself when things happen. I know that I am not a hundred percent all the time. I know that it's possible that if I had gone the extra mile or gone to this client there or done a better job on this pleading or whatever, the outcome might have been different, but I don't—maybe this is just ignorant hubris, but I don't believe that, number one. And number two, I don't let myself go there really."

He talks for a while about the irrationality of the existing system, all those procedural rules that don't always make sense—a reality Simon finds frustrating, depressing, and above all, maddening: "I get very angry, and I've been . . . I live off the anger at that, probably—feed off of it in terms of my writing, my working."

As we talk further, I can't quite let go of the image of that labyrinth and my curiosity about what it looks like to an attorney just starting out, or what it is like now after so many years.

"I wonder if it was daunting . . ." I begin.

No, I'm telling you—if there's any sort of serious character flaw that I have that really comes into play here, it would be, you know, sort of self-confidence that really goes sometimes toward arrogance or hubris. I don't really think that's who I am, what I am. I think I'm very aware of my own limitations. But at least in public, in persona, I try to project, and I guess I try to feel that as much as I can.

His tone suggests laughter at himself more than irritation at me for asking the question again, but still I remind myself to be careful what I assume. Just because I imagine I would find that labyrinth daunting doesn't mean he did, or does. He's telling me that's not how it is, so I drop the question. We move on to other things, stories of cases, reflections about how capital defense has changed over the years, and his own wrestling, periodically, with whether to stay in this work or maybe find a way to ease out of it. He starts to tell about a particularly challenging case he worked on, one that consumed a large part of his life for several years—and one that ended, rather miraculously, in a relative victory: a life sentence rather than death.

"I remember getting in the car and driving home [after getting that good news]," Simon begins, looking into the distance, "and I literally out loud said, 'You don't have to do this anymore. You don't have to do this anymore.'" His voice shakes a little, repeating those words. Then, coming out of the memory, he looks back at me and asks, "Now, what does that say?" I see him taking up the question, asking himself for the first time why those words had come to him in the wake of momentous good news.

> I know part of it was saying to me, You don't have to prove yourself anymore. You know: if ever there was a victory you could claim, this would be one. Because, like I was describing earlier, but for that initial honeymoon of victories, it's been just total and almost a hundred percent loss. There've been two or three victories, but basically everything I've worked on, the clients have, you know, not survived. It's really been tough. So—maybe part of it was saying to myself, OK, it's *not* your fault—

He laughs harshly and then stops abruptly, overtaken by tears. For several moments, neither of us speaks. When he does continue, his voice breaks on almost every word. "But part of it I think was just saying, That was a massive undertaking. It turned out well, thank goodness, and you gave more than, really, you should have, in terms of your life and every-thing, so it's OK to move on."

There is so much here, in this moment, these insights, that I hardly know what thought to offer first. But Simon moves on before we acknowl-edge what happened for him just then, how abruptly he stumbled into that chasm—letting himself off the hook for something he had just de-clared he didn't blame himself for in the first place.

I make the effort to follow his lead and attend to the other things he's now talking about, but all the while I'm thinking about that moment of realization, holding it in my mind, wondering if he will come back to it or if I should be the one to bring it up. I'm thinking about how he began by talking about winning—an honest-to-God victory that he could un-equivocally claim—and how, in order to show me exactly how notable an occasion that was, he contrasted it with the years of losses, the clients who have not survived. In trying to give some context for the good news, he instead took himself back to the bad and was suddenly left beholding *that* accumulation rather than the victory that he had started out describing. It caught both of us by surprise, but as I think about it now, I wonder if my original question ("I wonder if it was daunting?") somehow laid the groundwork for this—as though, while a part of him was telling me no, he didn't feel that, this other part, the part that needed to be told "it's not all your fault," was there under the surface, suddenly bursting forth.

About ten minutes later in the interview, as I'm listening and thinking about all this, Simon recalls the early years of his career.

"See, if we'd had this interview twenty-five years ago, I would be all self-righteous, and I would've been telling you I do this as a calling, and how you survive is because I just feel so morally right about it, and when you're doing what you know is right, that drives you, and all that. You know, it's not that I don't think all that anymore. I do. I mean, again, I go back to my pride—" He breaks off, distracted by another thought.

"It's funny, I just saw something as we were chatting." He apologizes for bouncing from topic to topic, but he doesn't want to forget what has just caught his attention. He slows down, almost as if he's deciphering the thoughts as he voices them.

"I was telling you at the beginning that I had all this hubris and confidence, and then I just realized I was saying"—he pauses and makes a sound that is not quite laughter—"that I had this very profound moment that led me to say, It's OK. It's not all your fault."

He looks at me, almost in wonder, as I nod and tell him I know, I'd seen that, I was considering whether to bring it up.

"So it's like, what's up with *that?*" he asks in a kind of amazement, trying to understand this apparent contradiction.

"Does it surprise you to see that?" It's obvious that it does; I think I'm just fumbling for something to say.

He nods, now crying hard. Somehow, unlike the moment just ten minutes ago, it feels as if he now acknowledges the tears, we acknowledge them together, and he is now ready to look at what he's just discovered. His voice is still thick as he explains, "It's the difference between what I know in my mind, my head, and what I internalize."

"Exactly."

We sit, quiet, for several moments. I think about his saying, "I don't let myself go there really." So often it's not a matter of what is true or untrue, but of what we can let ourselves know. The clues were there, if I think about it, in his original words: "persona," "I try to feel," "I don't let myself go there." Even as he was describing his undaunted confidence, this self-blame was there too—not necessarily more true or more real, but certainly less explicitly known.

"So, there's an impact!" Simon says, gathering himself and resuming the conversation. He had focused at the start on my interest in the impact of capital defense work, and when he returns to that phrase now, it's as if he's offering up this recent revelation. When he continues, it feels as if he is thinking this through for himself while, simultaneously, we are collaborating on the project of understanding his range of experience.

"So I guess one impact would be—that we've just revealed—is that at least *I* take on responsibility for a lot more than I probably should, right? In terms of who's responsible for outcomes, for what happens in cases."

"Who is? It's hard to know, huh?"

"Yeah, I mean, we could sit here and talk, and I could tell you what I know is, quote, 'true,' and I could definitely put fault in any number of places, but somehow it's clear, too, that I am irrationally—and I guess for me it's somewhat imperceptibly—putting myself right in the center of it. There you have it!" he concludes, shaking his head a little at the blatant truth. He had felt it too deeply, seen it too clearly, to pretend otherwise. It was not something he had walked in knowing, but now having visited this region of his emotional landscape, he would not deny it was there.

It's such a familiar human tale: if damage has been done, if terrible things have happened, we imagine ourselves part of the cause. A child blames herself for her parents' divorce. The brother of a murder victim, learning that his sister's attackers lured her away after she pulled over to the side of the road, is convinced that she had car trouble because he had neglected to check her engine when she'd asked him the day before. These are the meanings we make for ourselves, the stories we create in order to under-stand what went wrong. And if by any reckoning we actually *were* in a position of responsibility relative to the event, it is that much harder to construct a meaning that acknowledges but doesn't exaggerate that re-sponsibility. Adam's analogy to the rescue workers in the news story cap-tures this feeling: Your job was to save a life, and you didn't. Does that mean the execution was your fault, your failure?

Capital defenders know that it doesn't mean this—they know it in a real way, a believable way, with an understanding that has been forged out of a lot of tough and painful experience. But right alongside that, not precisely in contradiction to it but perhaps in companionship with it, they can feel the impact of the losses in a way that puts the blame on the limits of their own human capacity. If this latter feeling is harder to acknowledge, it may be because it's so painful, or because it doesn't match what they want to believe or what they recognize as necessary in order to persevere.

Later in our interview I ask Simon if he had experienced any inkling of these feelings of self-blame at the time when each loss occurred. "It's hard to say," he answers. "I've felt sadness, overwhelming grief, and just utter sort of despair and angst and confusion when I've lost clients." He pauses to think for a moment. "You know, it's funny. It's almost like— what's the analogy I'm looking for—it's like one of those things you really can't see directly, you can only see in the mirror." Obviously, he goes on to say, he *has* internalized the losses and in some way blamed himself for them, but looking back, he doesn't see himself as being aware of that feel-ing at the time. "Maybe it's just that I haven't let myself do that."

Now, finally, he had let himself. The interview had served as a kind of mirror, just as the news story had for Adam, showing him something that had been hard to apprehend straight on.

# CHAPTER 4

# The Fighting

MID-WAY THROUGH HIS career as a capital defense attorney, Nick was diagnosed with cancer. He had seen himself as being in the business of trying to save lives; now his own life needed saving. He's healthy now, but the cancer gave him a glimpse of mortality—and it showed him with renewed clarity what his work was about. "We need to be able to do for our clients what you did for me," Nick said to his oncologist as he thanked him at the end of the treatment.

How does he describe what his oncologist did? "It was: You come in, you take control, we can do this. Although you know it's dire, it's very positive: we're going to do these things."

It's dire, but here's what we're going to do. It's a reassuring taking-the-situation-in-hand that doesn't sugarcoat the reality but also doesn't leave the patient—or the client—alone with terror and helplessness, either. Indeed, it's a stance *against* helplessness. Facing a death sentence or, even more urgently, an execution date, the client, the client's family, and even in some sense the people protesting the death penalty look to the capital defender to provide this buffer and this focused hope. The situation is dire, but capital defenders, with their specific training, have the ability to figure out what to do and then do it.

In fact, the desire *not* to be helpless or impotent can be part of what propels capital defenders into the work in the first place. Before he got his law license, Adam stood with other protesters outside the prison during an execution. "I remember feeling so angry about the fact that the state was killing somebody, and we were singing 'Kumbaya' and burning candles. The last thing I felt was peace-loving," he says, shaking his head. "The idea that all we can do is hold a candle—"

Adam wanted more tools, a greater ability to get in there with something to do, something that might actually be able to stop the execution. In some essential way, wanting to be a capital defender means wanting to get into the fight. Several of the defenders I interviewed invoked the David and Goliath story—not surprising, as it's the standard parable of a scrappy and seemingly ill-equipped fighter defeating a mightier foe. What I realized when I reread the story, though, is that David actually volunteers for the challenge. He wants to attempt this seemingly impossible thing. It exactly aligns with the way Tim describes capital defense: at some level you have to feel, "I would love to be the one getting in that fight and slaying that giant."

So they get in the fight. They do what they can do. They don't let the long odds scare them into giving up or turning away, but those long odds are there, hovering in their peripheral vision or maybe right at the center. It's hard to say, hard to pin this down exactly. As they describe it, they know, yet don't want to fully know, how unlikely a win is.

"You don't lie," Nick says to me, trying to describe the complexity of meeting with clients on death row. "But you say, This is how we're going to fight this; these are the things we're going to do. . . . In that situation, you've got to have some hope. I would not want to sit there with no hope."

"Do you ever feel it differently from how you're presenting it?" I ask. "Do you ever feel as if there's less chance than you're . . . ?"

"Yeah. Oh, definitely. There *is* less hope. I mean, when somebody comes to me, post-conviction, the chances of winning are slim."

The chances are slim when a client has already been sentenced to death. Nick knows it, and the client must know it too. But I don't see Nick as misleading his clients, putting on a false front. He's too straightforward for that, and the complex texture of his interactions with clients in this regard becomes more apparent as he describes it further.

"The thing I tell everybody is, I can't make any guarantees. The only guarantee I can make to you is that I will work hard." He tells them that up front, and then he goes on to outline the legal issues that he believes are reasonable and the plans he has for litigating them. "I don't think I mislead them, but I'm sort of a cheerleader along the way. It's like, It's bad, but it's not beyond all hope."

I listen to him and think, isn't that what someone sitting on death row would want? Otherwise, what would be the difference between having an attorney at that point and not having one? If the person with the tools to litigate doesn't come in and say, "It's a long shot, but here's what I'm going to try," wouldn't it be like giving up before one had even begun the battle?

But every time Nick tells me what he tells the clients, I persist with my questions about what he himself is feeling at the same time. So when he tells me that he conveys to clients that the situation is not beyond all hope, I ask,

"Are you telling yourself that too? How does it live inside you, that sense of the odds?"

"Well, I don't know." He pauses to think a moment. "I think, in order to be a defense attorney, but a capital defense attorney probably even more so—you actually start to believe it. You believe you've got the winning claim, that there's no reason you shouldn't win. So I guess you do delude yourself."

Is it deluding oneself? It seems to me that awareness of the odds and hope of overcoming them exist simultaneously—and sometimes, in order for the attorney to persevere, the hope has to feel like actual belief. Gabe summarizes it vividly:

I think in order to do the work you have to believe that you can win. Because if you went in to every case thinking, I'm probably going to lose, but I'll see what I can do, you would be so demoralized that you wouldn't last very long. You would have no reason to do all of the things that are required of you. Like when the court sets a deadline so that you have to do five years of work in three months. You're called on to do extraordinary things sometimes, and I don't think that you could do that if you didn't have some extreme motivation to do it and also think that it might make a difference: I could win this, I could stop this. You know, you have to have that hope to get up and go do it every day.

*You have to have that hope.* There is both humor and poignancy in the rueful way the attorneys describe hope's stubborn persistence. On the one hand, I can see hope as something they cultivate in order to keep going, as Gabe suggests. On the other hand, hope also comes across as a sort of inevitable by-product or side effect, a dynamic they can recognize in themselves but not necessarily escape.

> You've got a hopeless case, but no matter how hopeless it is, when you get through writing the brief, you're convinced you're going to win. You know that's what's happening, but you still believe it! –Caroline

> I think I've always got a little bit of hope, or it wouldn't hurt so badly when [the courts] say no. You've always convinced yourself a little bit, even against all odds, this might work. You have to do that to write it well, to argue it well. If you don't believe your argument, you can't have a hope of winning. –Pamela

> Whenever you've got something filed, you tend to believe in what you've done. You think you're right, and there's always this feeling that you're going to get a stay, but then it always happens that you don't. Well, not always. I've had quite a bit of success getting stays in crisis cases. But still the majority are not going to happen. But you always do believe. –Eric

> [Clients] always hope when there's something pending. As do I, despite all odds and experience. You always hope. –Karen

A further complication is that the attorneys aren't just carrying hope on their own behalf. They also feel an obligation to be bearers of hope for their clients. Nick says, "I will never tell them there's no hope. I will tell them it's a difficult road—"

He trails off, but the implication is clear: it's a difficult road, but not over 'til it's over. You can file a last-minute pleading that almost feels like a waste of time, but "you can't risk that it's not," Nick says. The odds are long, but that last-minute effort might in fact work, "so you've got to try everything you can."

As a responsible attorney, you must try, and in one crucial way, offering hope seems like offering a desperately needed buffer between the client and the pending execution. But the question also arises: is so much hope ever at odds with the need to prepare for the execution if in fact it happens?

Julian tries to account for this by saying to clients, "I'm going to file a petition on your behalf. There's a minimal chance that it might work, but the chance is so slim that you should be doing all you need to do to prepare for dying, including meeting with everyone you need to see and saying everything you need to say."

There are echoes of Nick's oncologist analogy here: you explain what you're trying, but you don't evade the subject of death either. Done well, it strikes me as probably the best mix that anyone can offer in such a situation, but I can also see the inherent incompatibility of hoping for a stay and preparing for an execution. Julian goes on to say that he recognizes that no matter how slim he might describe the chance, just the mention of it, just the fact of his filing the petition, inevitably ignites hope. And again the question is whether this is emotionally helpful or harmful. Julian continues, "One of the harder things to bear, too, is that anything you do instills hope in family members and friends of your client. No matter how hopeless you portray the situation to them, as well. So it feels like when the execution occurs they have been blindsided, no matter how much you prepared them beforehand."

Listening to him, I wonder if the attorneys are not at some level blindsided, too, no matter how much they have prepared themselves.

It's not always the attorney who suggests that the client should be preparing for the execution. Often enough, clients are keenly aware of the prospect, so much so that their emotional needs may conflict with their attorneys' needs. "I've had people say to me, 'I want to know what's coming, I want to prepare myself, and I don't want to be thinking about the possibility of a last-minute stay,'" Gabe says, recalling clients who have told him that they would prefer he *not* file any kind of eleventh-hour petition that isn't likely to work but that will keep hope simmering.

I ask Gabe what goes through his mind at such times.

"There's a part of me that feels like—I mean, if somebody feels like they're ready to go, and I don't feel like they're passing up anything—"

He doesn't complete the sentence, but I understand what he's implying: he can accept clients' reluctance to have anything else filed if they've come to a point where they're ready to die *and* if they're not forgoing a chance that Gabe, as their attorney, thinks might be viable. A client might say, for example, that Gabe shouldn't bother to file a clemency petition, a step that is generally recognized as the last and least likely to work. If a client doesn't want that long-shot chance to compete with his or her own internal preparation for death, Gabe understands. "But it's hard," he concludes. "It's hard to run out of things to do."

Other attorneys acknowledge this tension as well. As we talk about it, Caroline wonders if some attorneys at the very end stage of a case file petitions that are such long shots that they might almost be classified as "frivolous" claims. "I think a lot of times lawyers do it for themselves," she says reflectively. That can be dangerous if taken too far, Caroline says, because attorneys might make judgments based on their own need to keep going rather than on what is actually the best thing to do. But the problem is, as Caroline explains, "You never get to the point where you want to stop. You never want to get to the point where you acknowledge that I've done all I can, because that means it's over."

So immersed in fighting until the end, so determined to see themselves as doing all that can be done, the attorneys may at times find it hard to let go of the search for the next possible step. What sometimes happens in such situations is that the client says, in effect, "You go ahead and fight, and I'll get ready in case we lose." Paul remembers a client with whom he was reviewing the last round of litigation saying outright, "If you want to do it, if it's important to you, then do it." The client acknowledged Paul's need to keep fighting, but on the day of the scheduled execution, when Paul was on the phone telling his client the latest news and outlining a possible next approach, the client finally said, "That's enough. Don't do any more. Just come on back here." Paul stopped what he was doing and got to the prison in time to say goodbye.

Sometimes, agonizingly, it happens the other way: the attorney has to announce that there's nothing left to do, and the client seems unable to accept that reality. Eric worked for a time in an office that got a lot of desperate requests from death row prisoners asking for legal help after most of the usual steps had already been taken. He remembers visiting one of these prisoners.

"He was begging, begging for us to do something. That was definitely the most difficult experience I've had. There's nothing more awful than telling somebody there's nothing you can do for them."

"What's going through your mind as you're hearing that?" I ask.

"Trying to figure out what you can do or say to—you know, you want to be able to do something that puts their mind at ease and gives them something. I can't imagine just waiting for your execution date without anything standing between you and that. So you look for something you can do. Even though you know it's essentially futile."

"Gives them something," I say, repeating Eric's phrase, "and gives you something, too, I'm thinking."

"Yeah, so I don't have to walk out not having done anything. I don't know if I could ever do that."

Yet sometimes a case reaches a point at which you do have to walk out, or walk away, with nothing left to try. Caroline remembers a case early in her career where she had to call the client and say that there was nothing else. "I called him up, and he said, 'I don't understand. I trusted you. I don't understand why this is going to happen.' That was just—aagh. He was so childlike. It was like, I trusted that you could do this, and you didn't do it."

"What did you say to him?" I ask, trying to fathom what could be said in such a conversation.

"I just said, 'I'm sorry. I wish I could do more.'"

Karen recounts a similar story of a client with an intellectual disability who was about to be executed and was utterly distraught, unable to accept what was coming.

"And I couldn't offer him anything," Karen says quietly. "It was *horrible*. He was too impaired, too distraught and angry and confused. In his mind—he was very childlike, and I think he felt like—legitimately so—he shouldn't be executed."

This was after the US Supreme Court had ruled executions of people with intellectual disabilities unconstitutional. I ask Karen how the case had gotten to this point.

"I came into the case after another lawyer had already screwed it up," Karen explains. I hear weariness more than anger in her voice. "We got a stay of execution, went through another round of litigation, and then they set another date. I did everything I could. We were litigating in every possible realm." She falls silent, and she seems to be replaying the scene in her mind.

"He just couldn't—there was no way for him to understand that. He came to trust me at a certain point, but then I think he felt like I had betrayed him because I couldn't keep him from being executed."

There are so many variations on this painful theme. Paul tells a story that is in one sense different from Karen's example: by the last day of the client's life, he was neither angry with his attorney nor pleading for something else to be done. Paul arrived at the prison, knowing the execution was twenty-four hours away, and found his client sitting with his family and singing hymns. "At a time when people could be very angry," Paul says slowly, "these folks were just transcendent. They had transcended the devastation that was upon them." He pauses a moment, and we sit with that image: he with the vivid memory of it, I with the picture he has given me through his telling. Then his tone changes, "But I didn't feel any better about it."

In addition to the feeling that would accompany any visit to a client twenty-four hours before an execution, Paul was disturbed about how some of the evidence in the case had been handled; there were unanswered questions that frustrate and nag him even years later. Walking away from that last visit, once his thoughts turned back to the case itself, he was furious all over again. "I was really angry about the way the evidence had been dealt with. And I guess I realized that—" He stops to take a deep breath and phrase the thought.

> I began to feel like the prosecutors and courts would do anything they could—not whether they were bound by any truth, but just anything they could think of—to assure that people were executed. I'd certainly understood the zeal that prosecutors had, before that. I'd been involved with a number of cases and had won some and lost others and certainly had seen them fight hard, but this seemed to me to be different. It was, No matter what you do, we're going to get you. I was not only angry, but I felt more helpless than I'd ever felt before.

Helplessness is the dominant emotion in these accounts. "I'm there with her, and I have to tell her I can't stop it," Sebastian recalls, describing his visit just hours before the execution of a client he had represented for many years. "It was one of the toughest things I ever had to do. Actually, I think it was harder on me than it was on her. She knew it was coming. She was resigned to it. But I'm the one who had to fucking *say*—I mean, you've put your trust in me, I'm your representative, and I have to say, I can't stop it."

These are stories of attorneys coming up against the limits of their power. The skills, the training, the particular kind of willingness to jump into the fight—all of this distinguishes them from others who also may not want the execution to happen, but all of it only goes so far. Sometimes the limits are glaringly, agonizingly apparent. In describing what it feels like when a client gets an execution date, a few attorneys compare it to seeing someone tied to the tracks as a train approaches. This image illustrates something that is not quite captured by either the oncologist or the David and Goliath analogies: how desperately threatening the whole thing can feel. Capital defenders come in ready to help, even driven to help, but sometimes they are made acutely aware of their helplessness. As Benjamin wryly explains,

> It's not like you're a great surgeon, and they bring you to a clean operating room with someone who is at death's door, and you get to do the work. It's more like, you get that scenario, but there's another surgeon in the room who's trying to kill the patient while you're trying to save him. So you're constantly coming to blows with this other person who's trying to kill the patient while you're trying to save him, and you have no idea that they're not going to knock you backwards over a crash cart and kill the person while you can't react. It's out of your hands.

So many of the attorneys use the phrase "a life is in your hands," yet here Benjamin offers this paradoxical counterpoint: saving the life is your responsibility but also out of your control. "Learning to accept that has been the toughest part of being a death penalty defense lawyer, for me," he says.

Benjamin compared a capital defender's experience to a surgeon's, as Nick had compared it to an oncologist's. In rereading surgeon Atul Gawande's essay "On Fighting" from his book *Better* (New York: Picador, 2007, 161), I was struck by his comment that the hardest part of being a doctor is not mastering the necessary skills but being able "to know what you have power over and what you don't." Later in that essay, Gawande makes this observation: "The seemingly easiest and most sensible rule for a doctor to follow is: Always Fight. Always look for what more you could do. I am sympathetic to this rule. It gives us our best chance of avoiding the worst error of all—giving up on someone we could have helped."

As heard in so many of these attorneys' comments, "always fight" could be the motto of capital defense as well. But following that guiding principle doesn't exempt attorneys (and doctors) from uncertainty or helplessness. And it's safe to say that capital defenders receive far less public respect for their persistence than doctors do. To continue Benjamin's metaphor: not only are the attorneys coming to blows with others who are trying to kill their patients, but most onlookers can't fathom why they are so determined to save these particular patients in the first place.

Julian has decided that he will never witness an execution. This is a question that comes up among capital defenders; some have witnessed, some have not, and various considerations influence the decision. For Julian, one of the considerations is that witnessing would feel like a greater concession of defeat than he wants to make.

"It's not wrong, if you've exhausted everything you can do to try to save somebody, it's not wrong to be there," he begins. "But there's something really out of sync about being the person who's charged with trying to save the life of the person they're killing, and just *sitting* there, just putting your butt down on the chair and watching them kill your client. It's absurd to me."

"It would feel to you like, 'I should be doing something'?"

"Well, no, it's—" He stops to consider how to show me what he means. "It's demeaning. It's a violation of my dignity, which I won't permit. It's an emasculation and, you know, a complete statement of disempowerment, and—it's just not going to happen."

I nod at the clarity, the drawing of a personal line. I hadn't understood it in exactly this way before. Gaining momentum, Julian continues,

> [It's like they're saying,] You're powerless to save this person, and we're going to kill him. It's, it's just—they're turning your client into an inanimate object. They're treating your client as though your client is nothing, and by proxy you are nothing. That's an assault on

your dignity, and so, it's like—I guess I'm willing to tilt at windmills all the way to the end. I'm willing to fight even though there's nothing left to win, but I'm not willing to put myself in a place where I concede my powerlessness, even though that's what I am: powerless.

I know some attorneys see the witnessing issue differently, but here, I am less struck by the dilemma itself than by the overarching considerations of power, dignity, and identity. Julian's resolution about not wanting to witness an execution shows me so much about the personal reckoning each attorney must undergo: What am I willing and unwilling to do? What feels like fight, and what feels like surrender?

Issues of surrender and dignity came up for Elliot the first time he submitted a clemency petition for a client. Seeking clemency from a governor is understood as a last-resort act, the final strategy to try after all rounds of litigation are over. (For someone on death row, clemency grants life but not liberty; it commutes a death sentence to life in prison.) Elliot tells me that he knows clemency is rare—"an act of grace" is how he describes it—and that it is often granted at political cost. But still, he hates the clemency process because of how demeaning it feels. He says that submitting that first clemency petition was the point at which "it felt like I changed from a fighter to a beggar."

There's the heart of it. One can be proud of fighting but ashamed of begging.

"Maybe it was that I couldn't define myself in opposition to something else anymore," Elliot continues. "It was no longer adversarial . . . it was just us sitting there saying please. It just felt undignified and humiliating in a way that nothing else—I mean, when the [federal appeals court] was yelling at us, it didn't feel demeaning, but that part, the clemency part, that was the place that tipped the balance or crossed over for me."

"It's a more supplicating stance," I suggest.

"It really is. That's right."

The kind of dignity that the attorneys experience in the role of fighter—David stepping in to take on the giant—is missing when they feel forced to assume these more demeaning postures: begging, watching helplessly while the thing they tried to prevent is now being carried out. Again, I come back to their image of watching someone tied to the tracks as the train approaches. Though the odds are long by the post-conviction stage of capital litigation, for much of the time the attorneys can feel as if they are frantically working to slow the train down or to untie the knots so that the person is no longer directly in harm's way. When none of this works, and the train is fast approaching, *and* they are forced to stand there and watch the collision, the feeling of helplessness can be close to unbearable. Everything in them cries out for action, and yet they are now required to be still.

Keith remembers the necessarily repressed fury that he felt as he witnessed a client's execution for the first time. Seated in front of him in the witness area were the district attorney and the detective on the case, both of whom, in Keith's estimation, had acted unjustly and dishonestly throughout the legal proceedings.

> So here you are with the two people responsible for derailing justice, and you can't object, you can't argue, there's nothing for you to do. Every part of you wants to just whale, just physically whale on them. I wanted to attack them. I mean, the crudest part of me wanted to just attack them. The professional part of me wanted to stop them, wanted to do something, wanted to file something, object, *do something*. But all you can do is just sit and watch. I mean, you can't say anything, you can't do anything, you just sit and watch this happen to your client. There's just nothing more helpless than that.

When they are possessed by the impulse to intervene but, as Caroline puts it, unable to do anything "but just let it happen," it ends up feeling "surreal," a description that reminds me of Julian's saying that it would feel absurd to have to sit passively and watch.

"I remember thinking about the fact that I could understand people doing dramatic, illegal things to try to stop it," Caroline says to me, recalling some of her early experiences with clients' executions. "I mean, you know you can't, but I could understand the things that somebody might want to do. In the way that people do when they're in a war and trying to protect people, or when their family's threatened—the instinct to survive and to protect people you care about. I do really think that it's just a human instinct."

Isabel speaks similarly. Describing last visits with clients, the visits that happen just before an execution, she says, "This is the point at which you want to call in the SWAT team, but we're only lawyers. We can't lay on the tracks and stop the train."

*We're only lawyers*. This is the paradox. Lawyers have more tools to intervene with than many others do, but when an execution is coming like a train barreling down the tracks, those tools can feel painfully insufficient.

The feeling of not wanting to surrender or concede, even when the immediate battle has been lost, may be part of what propels some attorneys to go into their offices right after an execution rather than allowing themselves any kind of break. "It's a stupid little thing," Roger says, "but I'm going to go to work every day afterwards because I'm not going to let them beat me. I mean, I may not stay there all day, I may leave at lunchtime—"

He laughs, acknowledging that some days, some times, showing up at the office right after an execution may be a symbolic act more than an effective one, the fighter dragging himself up from the mat even though he actually needs a break before he'll be ready to go another round. But even though Roger characterizes this habit as "a stupid little thing"—perhaps expressing sheepishness about how much the symbolic value of the act matters to him—I feel the deeper resonance of what he's doing. He's maintaining his sense of himself as a fighter even when he's hurting.

Nick puts it similarly: "You can't let the state know they got to you." This is why he has never taken a day off, he explains. "It's like, You're not going to beat me down. I will go back the next day."

Listening to these kinds of comments, I find myself wondering whether "the state" would necessarily know if it had gotten to these attorneys. It's an oddly faceless Goliath that these Davids are fighting, and in a strict sense perhaps nobody would notice if they needed to retreat for a while after a loss. But they themselves would be watching. This is a way of talking back to the helplessness, even defying it.

As hard as it can be to tolerate their own helplessness, witnessing the helplessness of others close to the execution may be even harder. Julian spoke of this when he described the difficulty of instilling hope in clients' family members and then feeling as if that leaves them blindsided by the execution. When executions do happen, the anguish of clients' surviving family members can be overwhelming.

One scene in particular stays with Roger. A client was scheduled for execution. Roger got to the prison about fifteen minutes before the end of visitation, just enough time to say a brief goodbye to the client, who was having a last visit with his mother. The guards told them the visit was over. Roger and the client's mother walked out of the prison, knowing that as they were leaving, the client was being taken to the execution chamber. They walked through the prison gate into a blisteringly hot day.

> We were standing on this burning blacktop, you know how the parking lot gets, the sun's beating down, and I'm there with the minister and [my client's] mother, who's hunched over, and she is just—broken down. Sobbing, delirious, you know; she's just said goodbye to her son for the last time. That was one of the hardest moments. And, you know, that's the thing about the death penalty that people don't see. It was just brutal. I remember that scene so vividly. What can you do? You can't leave, and you can't change anything. You can't do anything for her.

*You can't do anything for her.* It's that abject powerlessness in the face of someone else's agony that is so vivid for Roger, and for Caroline, too, in the memory she recounts to me as she tries to explain why one particular experience of witnessing an execution was distinctly difficult.

The witness area at an execution is usually divided so that witnesses who have been involved with the prisoner sit separately from those related to the victim of the prisoner's crime. This time, Caroline and the prisoner's brother were the only ones there for the man about to be executed. They sat together and reached out to hold one another's hands as the execution proceeded. Caroline's voice breaks as she describes this, and it already sounds so difficult that I assume this is the hard part of the story. But she hasn't even gotten to the worst of it.

By coincidence, Caroline and the brother were staying in adjacent rooms at the nearby motel. When they got back to the motel after the execution, Caroline could hear the brother next door, alone and sobbing.

Caroline can hardly get through the telling of this.

"It just brought home *his* helplessness. It's one of the saddest things I remember." In another moment she adds, "Because you can imagine, in order for [me] to hear it, he was just—"

As the memory again rips through Caroline and leaves her unable to speak, I can indeed imagine it, the terrible sound of those sobs loud enough for someone in another room to overhear. Caroline says she didn't feel she knew the brother well enough to intrude on his private grief, so she stayed on her side of the wall. But the memory of that night is indelible.

Recounting his experience with his client's mother, Roger said that this was one of the things about the death penalty that people don't see. I feel something like that as I replay this moment with Caroline in my mind. These occasions of helplessness, this lasting empathetic grief, so vivid for the attorneys even years later, so palpable to me as I sit with them—this, too, is something about the death penalty that people don't see.

We're taught to believe that there's some relationship between effort and achievement. Working hard at something, working *well* at something, should count in some way. It should make a difference. A challenge for capital defenders is that their experience seems to keep disproving this. "You are taught as a lawyer: if you do your job and you do a good job for your client, you can win," Isabel says wryly. "What you realize is that it doesn't matter how good a job you do, you're not going to win. It's a tremendous feeling of helplessness: I'm doing everything right. I'm doing my job, I'm doing my job *really well*, and my client is still getting executed. It's an exercise in futility."

So law school, in that sense, doesn't prepare attorneys for capital defense. Simon observes that this lack of connection between effort and reward can be a particularly tough challenge for high-achievers who are accustomed to a correlation between the two.

> It usually doesn't matter how good you are or how well you do in a case. No matter how hard you work, for the most part you lose. No matter how well-crafted your pleadings, you lose. No matter how correct your arguments are, courts either change the rules or just ignore them, and no one holds them accountable. You can file the most brilliant pleadings based on thousands of human hours of effort and get denied, or you can file a one-issue piece of crap and get denied. It's usually the same result in front of most of the courts in the death belt. This phenomenon makes this work very difficult for high-achieving, smart, talented attorneys. Big law firm lawyers whom we get to do these cases sometimes really struggle with this. We all do, of course, but I guess those of us in it for good have either just gotten used to it, or gotten real cynical, or internalized the losses, or all of the above.

Even if they've gotten used to it, they acknowledge the corrosive effects of this apparent lack of connection between skill (or effort) and outcome. Looking back over his own track record in post-conviction capital work, Benjamin recalls that after a couple of early wins, he then didn't win another case—in the sense of preventing an execution—for several years. When he did win, it was "incredibly satisfying but also misleading."

"Misleading in what sense?" I ask.

"I thought: I must have arrived, must have finally reached a level of skill where I am now capable of winning these cases," he explains.

"You thought there was a correlation between your skill and the outcome," I paraphrase.

"Right, exactly. You try to create a narrative where there's growth and meaning, as opposed to: this is just another random event that happened to break in your favor. [You tell yourself,] I should be better now, so if I continue to lose, it's got to be [for a reason other than that] I'm inexperienced. It's got to be, I've gained experience but I lack judgment, or I lack commitment, or whatever."

"Or else maybe there isn't a correlation," I suggest.

"That's right, and I think in my quieter moments, that is the truth, to the extent that there is a truth to be found at the heart of all this. It's that there is not any rhyme or reason to who wins and who loses. . . . It really doesn't have anything to do with the quality of your work."

"What's it like to realize that?"

"Deeply frustrating."

Elliot remembers the day it hit him that hard work was not necessarily going to make the difference. It was when he first understood that a particular client's execution was inevitable. "I always think of George Orwell's *Animal Farm*," he says. "There's Boxer, who was a horse, who says, 'Whenever there's a problem, I can work harder.' His solution to the problem is always 'I can work harder.' But eventually the pigs send him off to the glue factory; he's a very tragic character. So at that point the illusion that I can work harder evaporates."

Before I began interviewing capital defenders, I imagined that their experiences might be characterized by a greater feeling of agency, of power and ability to act, than others who likewise work against the death penalty but are comparatively limited by what they can do to stop any particular execution. When I ask the question that way, comparing the attorney's range of tools to stop an execution to, say, those of a client's family member or even those of death penalty protesters, they all agree that in that sense they do have more to work with. They *are* the ones who can come in with the legal skills comparable to, as Nick suggested, the medical skills of an oncologist and say, "Here's what we're going to do."

It's true enough that their skills, training, and access to specific kinds of interventions make them more directly able to help. But their investment of time, hope, and—simply—*themselves* in each case makes it hurt worse when they confront the limits of that ability. I heard more variations on this theme of helplessness and saw more evidence of how deeply and lastingly it affected them than I could have predicted at the outset.

Without the illusion that working harder necessarily yields a better result, why do these attorneys work as hard as they do? Here we're back to the "can't help but fight it" idea, so strongly felt at the beginning and so persistent even in the face of so much defeat. Something very deep and abiding in these attorneys still wants to engage in this fight.

But the periodic feelings of futility, the cynicism, and the internalized losses can all overtake them, especially at the toughest moments. And then because of this, any indication that others recognize their efforts can take them by surprise and sometimes even bring them to tears. Isabel remembers waiting while a client was being executed, a client to whom she had become quite close. Afterward, when the prison chaplain came out and spoke with her, Isabel asked how her client had been at the end and what he had said. The chaplain told Isabel that the client had voiced his appreciation for what Isabel had done and had said, "She's a fighter." Isabel remembers that at that point she started crying.

I saw this in other attorneys, or heard them refer to it: how moving it is when anyone, but above all a client, recognizes and appreciates them as a fighter—especially at those times when they feel as if they've been knocked to the mat.

Sometimes the final conversations between client and attorney happen over the telephone. Prisons schedule visiting hours up to a certain point before an execution, and then all visitors, including attorneys, are required to leave. But sometimes an attorney is allowed to be on the phone with the client after the visits close and even right up until moments before the execution gets underway.

Simon remembers talking with a client on one of those last phone calls, explaining what had just happened with the court, that their final legal effort had been denied. "I said something about, a bunch of fat white guys said he deserved to die—kind of just trying to make light of but communicate what had happened." Simon looks over at me, and I wonder if he's checking to see my reaction to an attempted joke under such circumstances. I just nod, but to myself I'm thinking that I completely understand the impulse. This is where the phrase "gallows humor" comes from, after all. But what's also true about extreme situations is that humor can turn to grief in a quick moment.

"Then I got emotional," Simon goes on. He speaks slowly, almost as if he's trying to get the words right in the recalling of them. "I was saying, 'I'm sorry I couldn't stop it,' and I'll never forget, he said, 'Now son, don't worry about it. It's OK. You did your best.'"

I know "son" is a common figure of speech, not necessarily meant literally, but it's impossible for me to hear it and not think of Simon's comments earlier in our conversation about how his own father never believed in his work as a capital defense attorney. I don't want to interrupt the story, and for all I know this is just something I notice because it's a Southern idiom that my Northern ear can't help but catch, so I don't say anything right away. Simon continues, speaking through tears,

"And it just struck me, I mean, he was fathering me at the time and taking care of *me*—" He's crying fully now, and I don't think I'm imagining the personal impact of the comment after all.

"It's an incredible story," I say finally. "Incredible that he called you 'son.'"

"It was weird," he responds, nodding. "I remember when he said it—I mean, I know I was just experiencing him as comforting me, but I also remember sort of being struck by it too. I didn't say anything; I just accepted it, kept saying, 'I'm sorry.' It was right in the middle of that that he said, 'They're coming for me now. I've gotta go—'"

The waves in these stories just keep coming. Whenever I think I've heard the hardest thing, the rawest moment, I hear something more. "And that was it," Simon concludes, shaking his head.

*That was it.* The client was gone, and Simon, by almost any standard, was left feeling that once again his hard work hadn't made the crucial difference, hadn't been enough to save a life. But someone—and, stunningly, not just anyone, but the person most directly affected—had seen the essence of who Simon had hoped to be in this struggle: the one who did what he could do, fought as hard as he could fight.

Earlier I described Adam's feelings of frustration and impotence as he stood outside the prison holding a candle at a vigil as an execution was being carried out. At that time, not yet having worked as a capital defender, it was the relative powerlessness of that action that struck him. But years later, having gone through several clients' executions, he realized that he noticed whether there was a crowd of protesters when he came out afterward. Emerging from the prison after an execution "to a crowd of people who care about you, care about what you do, who are there to say with their bodies and their presence, We object to this"—all of that now makes a tremendous difference. In contrast, he says, "When you walk out and there's not a soul who appears to give a shit whether your client lived or died, it's a real different feeling. It's way, way worse. *Way* worse."

"You start to see those people with the candles in a different way," I say, and he nods.

"Exactly. Absolutely."

Once again, to be acknowledged, and in this case also to walk back out into a community of people who recognize what you've done and believe the fight is worthwhile, matters a great deal.

When Adam spoke earlier in our conversation about coming in at the end stage of a case and working day and night, "knowing that I'm going to lose," he concluded by saying simply, "But this is what we do."

What is it that they do? Tilt at windmills? Ante up repeatedly for a game that's rigged against them? Is it a fool's enterprise?

"What you're doing is you're making the state work like hell if it wants to take somebody's life," Adam explains at one point in our conversation. So this is part of it. If you can't always slay the giant, you can at least make him work like hell. If something is about to happen that you find morally repugnant, you can at least refuse to stand back and let it happen easily.

"It also sounds like you'd rather be the one fighting than not," I observe.

"Oh yeah," Adam agrees. "I am trained to do this, you know? I don't *know* that the next guy is trained as well as I am. I know lots of people who are better lawyers than me, and I'd be glad for them to do it, but they can't do 'em all, and I can't do 'em all, but I feel very confident in my ability to give my clients really top-of-the-line representation."

"I'm also thinking, if the choice for you personally is between fighting and not fighting, you would rather fight."

"Right. I chose this line of work for a reason."

Together we recall how Adam had said earlier that he couldn't bear the feeling of complicity that would arise if he knew executions were going on and he wasn't at least trying to prevent them.

The paradox for so many capital defenders is that, while they are too often hit by their own helplessness with respect to the death penalty, they also sense intuitively that they would feel worse, at least in this regard, if they didn't do the work they do. Atticus Finch, the fictional lawyer whom so many of these capital defenders invoke as a model, put it this way when explaining the meaning of courage to his daughter, Scout: "It's when you know you're licked before you begin but you begin anyway and you see it through no matter what."

I don't know if the capital defenders I spoke with would view themselves as courageous, but I suspect they recognize themselves in that line from *To Kill a Mockingbird*. This is who they want to be; this is the part they want to have played in the brutal story of the death penalty—to see it through no matter what. If death sentences are imposed, and executions are pending, and lives are threatened, then even though they may get knocked down repeatedly in the trying, most of the time they would rather be fighting than not.

# CHAPTER 5

# The Impact

WE'RE ABOUT AN hour into the interview. Paul has just been talking about the devastating weariness he feels after a client's execution, mixed with anger and repetitive nightmares in which there's something he's got to file, and he's trying to get to court but can't make it in time. He says the dreams sometimes recur for several nights in a row before they gradually subside.

I ask what doesn't subside. What stays with him?

"There's a sadness that never goes away," he says quietly. "I mean, it doesn't intrude into my consciousness when I'm just sort of living everyday life, but I think at some level beneath all of this there's an abiding sadness that's always there."

He can feel it when there's nothing to distract him from it, when he slows down and stops focusing on the next immediate thing he has to do. At times when he calms down and becomes reflective—like now—he can feel it: an underlying layer of sadness that has come to feel like a permanent part of him.

"I don't have to conjure it up," he says. "It has almost a physical presence."

It does. It's an undercurrent that I, too, feel as I sit with him and that I have felt during so many of these interviews.

"Can you say what it's like?" I ask him. "How you feel it physically?"

"I feel it in my stomach. Not nausea, not a knot. It's just a kind of uneasiness. It's the kind of thing that makes you want to take deep breaths and try to sort of relax, because it's the opposite of being relaxed. It's feeling a little shaky, a little unsteady. And sad."

I understand why he might fully notice this feeling only when he's not distracted by ordinary pressing demands. It makes me wonder if the reverse is also true: if one reason to keep so busy and so engaged with other things might be to keep from settling in to this place of sadness. I don't think that all his work is simply a way to avoid melancholy. Like everyone I interviewed, Paul always has enough to keep him legitimately, even urgently, busy every day; he doesn't need to manufacture distractions. But I tentatively suggest that maybe there's an inherent appeal in getting swept up by the immediate tasks and demands. Maybe at some level he does want to avoid really tuning in to this abiding sadness.

He nods. "It's not a terribly good place to be," he agrees.

I embarked on these interviews wanting to know how capital defenders are affected by their work, how it has gotten inside them and marked them in lasting ways. Everyone has stories—other people's, if not their own—of capital defenders drinking too much, smashing walls or beer bottles when bad news comes down, staying up until all hours, snapping at colleagues or their families because of the stress. All this creates a certain kind of picture, and if it isn't a picture of people *unaffected* by their work, it nevertheless fits a certain familiar image: the driven defense attorney working hard under pressure.

Underneath all this, though, is something else. Underneath the outward displays of frustration is, as Paul puts it, an abiding sadness that gets less notice than the stress and overwork. It's what is always there and what is most tempting to avoid. When Isabel mentions capital defenders' reputation for heavy drinking, I ask her, "What are people trying not to feel?" She answers immediately: "The grief. It's impossible to keep up with it," she says. "You haven't [dealt with the grief from] one execution, and you get hit with another."

Capital defenders are lawyers, but their work quickly becomes about much more than the law. It slams them right up against some of the rawest aspects of human experience, forcing them to rise to occasions for which no one could have prepared them.

Early in her career, Pamela visited a client whose execution was scheduled for the following morning. "We knew he was going to die," Pamela remembers. "He said, 'My execution is at 7:00 in the morning. Will you call me at 4:00?' I said, 'Of course.' I went home and set my alarm for 3:30, and then I thought, 'Oh my God, I cannot do this. I absolutely cannot make this phone call.' But I did."

"What was it like to do it?"

"It was just surreal. I can't talk to this man they're about to kill. I don't want to have to deal with that. I don't want to do it. I just thought, *I'm going to throw up. I'm scared.* It's—afraid you'll mess up, afraid you'll let him down. And I don't want it—you know, I don't want it in me. I don't want to have to."

*I don't want it in me.* Pamela felt an instinctive self-protective resistance to what she was about to do, but went ahead and did it anyway. It had to be done, and at that moment she was the one to do it. Again and again their work makes these kinds of demands so that, over time, whether they want it or not, raw and painful experiences are *in* these capital defenders, as Pamela so vividly describes it. As Karen says,

> The hardest thing, the crux of it, is what happens in those half hours of the last visit. That's the most emotional stuff for me, the most loaded, the stuff that puts me over the edge, the stuff that's the hardest to talk about. It's the experience with the individual clients. You're the last person they get to see, besides the guard. And you still can't touch them. You're trying to offer solace to somebody who's about to die. It's unbelievable. No one can be adequate in that situation. How could you possibly?

As impossible as it may be, this is a task capital defenders are often asked to perform. Not long after Gabe began work at a capital defense office, a colleague who was filing last-minute appeals in a case asked him to go to the prison and visit with the client so that somebody would be there if this was indeed the last night of his life.

"It was made easier in some ways," Gabe says as he begins to recount the story, "because the client had a really strong religious belief and had been on death row for 17 years and was firmly convinced that he was going to a better place. He didn't seem too nervous, but *I* was petrified."

I ask what especially scared him, and he replies,

> Well, I guess—there's no course in law school in bedside manner at an execution. I didn't really know—I was sent down there with not a lot of instruction about what to do, what to expect. . . . I knew the client, but I didn't know how he was going to be. I think that was part of it. I didn't know how he was going to be; I didn't know if he was going to be freaking out. I mean, I think it's hard not to imagine yourself in that person's position, and I would be terrified. And I'm supposed to be—I thought I had some responsibility to be a counselor or to, I don't know, I guess I didn't really know exactly what my role was, but I felt like I should be doing something to help him, but I didn't really feel like I knew what that was. I'd never done it before! I didn't have any words of—I had nothing, I felt like. I guess I was afraid he would need or want something from me that I wouldn't know how to give him, you know? Or that he would look to me for comfort and reassurance, and I was scared myself, so I didn't know if I could give him that. So, yeah, it was fear of the unknown, fear of being so close to a planned death.

*I wonder if any part of it was wondering whether you could handle it.*

> Yeah, I didn't want to freak out in there either. . . . There's a part of me that thinks if I had known beforehand, I probably would have tried to get out of it! You know what I mean? Because I was kind of thrown into it. And I understand it now, because I've had cases where I haven't been able to get up to the prison at execution time because I'm litigating to the very last minute, and so—but it is a kind of weird thing to send somebody else to do that. I understand,

from the lawyer's perspective, thinking, "I want somebody to be there with the client," but it's a hard thing to send somebody to do.

*What are the feelings that make you say, "If I'd known, I would have tried to get out of it"?*

It just—it felt a little traumatic. It's one thing knowing what's happening to people; it's another thing being there. . . . It was tremendously sad, it was tremendously ugly, I thought, and barbaric. And in a way it's hard not to feel like, at some point—and I think this is a feeling that other lawyers have struggled with as well—it's hard not to feel sort of a part of it in a way by being there.

Each attorney has to sort out, however imperfectly, what feels like complicity and what feels like protest—which may include wrestling with questions about the implications of participating in the death penalty system at all, as Gabe alludes to here. Meanwhile, as Gabe also suggests, attorneys are trying to manage their own fear or guilt or grief so that those feelings don't overwhelm their capacity to be available and helpful to the client. No wonder Karen's response, when I ask her what she tries to do during last visits with clients, is the deceptively simple, "Not be inadequate."

A huge part of what the attorneys feel the situation requires of them is that they handle or even conceal their own feelings so that the focus remains on the client's needs, whatever they might be at that time. Lou, who describes last conversations with clients as "gut-wrenching," remembers lying stretched out on the floor of a motel room talking on the phone with a client in the wee hours before a 7:00 a.m. execution. "I try to be strong, I try not to break down," he says of this and other such final conversations.

Isabel describes it like this:

You're just trying to hold it together. There's this tremendous cognitive dissonance: you're trying to appear calm and professional and somewhat comforting, "Let me tell you about the legal issues," and the other part of you is going, *Oh my God, this guy's about to fry.*

You're trying to separate the two parts of your psyche: how you're responding as a human being and how horrifying it is and [at the same time] trying to be this calm lawyer. You spend so much energy shutting this part of yourself down so that you can do this other part that you get to the point where you can't *not* be shut down anymore.

One day, after recently going through several clients' executions, Isabel attended a commemorative exhibit that would ordinarily have brought her to tears. "I realized that this was moving and that I might have cried before, but now, I don't do that anymore. I felt like, I can't cry. I'm numb."

Numbness—such a common human response when an experience is too intense or too overwhelming—comes up often as the attorneys try to describe the aftermath of clients' executions.

I was numb for a good while [after my first client's execution]. Just numb. –Keith

I think when executions have gone through, what I've felt is a devastating numbness. A complete sapping of energy. –Julian

I'm sure this is significant—I don't remember the emotions [associated with witnessing an execution for the first time]. It's like, when I think about it, it's like watching a movie. I've removed myself from it. –Caroline

I felt incapacitated for a while, after each execution. I couldn't move. My body felt very heavy. –Paul

I was just sort of numbed by the experience. I mean, I'd never seen anybody be killed before. I witnessed a murder. –Roger

Roger gives me an example of what numbness, shock, and a sense of remove from ordinary experience looked like one morning after he had witnessed a client's execution. He describes what happened when he tried to make himself breakfast: "I decided I was going to toast a bagel," he explains, laughing a little because it seems like such a simple thing. "And I burned three bagels to a blackened crisp because I just couldn't toast the bagel—I was distracted. I'd put one in and get distracted, and before I know it there's smoke coming out, so I'd put [in] another—this was three times!"

Hearing this story, I understand that the distraction Roger describes is different from the preoccupation he experiences when deep in the midst of writing legal material. Both might lead him to be less present in a domestic moment, but the preoccupation that comes from immersion in a challenging creative task seems very different from the numbness and distraction that Roger describes feeling that morning after the execution. "After that, I wasn't right for a good, long while," he goes on to say. "It was sort of a combination of shock and then just depression."

It can be hard to find words for exactly how it feels right after a client's execution.

"I have a now-familiar cycle post-execution, an emotional cycle," Karen begins.

I ask if she can describe it.

"It's hard to articulate. It's low-level depression and kind of a feeling of—"

She pauses, and I can feel her trying, really trying to put words to this familiar but immensely private experience.

"There's an emotional—" She breaks off again and repeats, "I've never tried to actually articulate it."

I feel myself almost holding my breath, hoping she will keep trying. She does, gathering momentum as she speaks.

You're laid out from the experience, emotionally you're laid out, and there's a kind of flattening. Underlying it is kind of—you're *wounded* in some way. I mean, it's a blow, obviously. And there's a little bit, I think, of—the ends get a little burnt off. It feels like flat affect, like exhaustion. No. Not flat affect resulting from exhaustion; it's *from* the ends being burnt off. It's just, it's so—I don't know. I think one doesn't know how to cope, so there's a little bit of just shutting down, and there's a little bit of survivor's guilt that happens—that has become a pretty familiar thing, like it takes a while to get your appetite back, like you shouldn't be enjoying a good meal, and yet at the same time there's a little bit where it's like: the sky is blue; the trees are green. You know, it's a very—a lot of opposites.

How long does this last? "Very intensely for at least three or four days," she responds. "And then it takes me a long time to get back into gear. I mean, partly it *is* just exhaustion, from working so hard. But it takes me a long time to get back up to speed, functioning in any sphere of my life at any full level. You just feel kind of muted."

They are grieving the loss of a human being, sometimes one to whom they have grown close, but that's not all of it. If you look up definitions of traumatic loss, you see that it's typically characterized by words like "sudden," "unanticipated," "outside of ordinary experience." An execution is ostensibly neither sudden nor unanticipated, yet most definitions of traumatic loss would include death that results from killing—from a person's life being deliberately taken.

The paradox of execution is that it is planned and (at least intellectually) anticipated, but it also involves a life deliberately taken in a way that, no matter how often one may have seen it, is outside of ordinary experience. Added to this, for capital defenders, is the complexity of having been in charge of trying to prevent the killing from taking place and believing they must now be strong and able to hold it together for others. When they feel "numbed," "flattened," or "muted," it is surely in response to all of this in addition to the loss of the specific individual.

Given that they work so hard to manage their emotions and not "freak out in there," not come across as needing solace, what happens when they can't quite do that and their own fear or grief or exhaustion shows through?

"I don't know if I hate it or if it's very rewarding," Nick says as he begins telling about what it's like to have last conversations with clients who are about to be executed. "You know, you're fighting back the tears when you're talking to them, because you don't want to—"

He leaves that sentence unfinished, but he goes on to say that it's also gratifying to be present for other human beings in the last hours of their lives. "It's rewarding that I can fulfill that role," Nick says, "though I don't necessarily *like* to."

I can see it: there's a certain brutal privilege in doing this for someone else, even if it's a terrible thing to have to do. As Nick explains further, the thing he doesn't want to do, the reason he works to fight back the tears, becomes clearer. He's telling about a last visit with a client to whom he had become especially attached and whose loss he was already dreading as they sat in the visiting room that last afternoon.

"I remember that day he was more worried about me than he was about his own situation," Nick says, shaking his head. As he told the client about the latest legal news, "[The client] was like, 'Hey, I'm worried about you.' I wasn't sleeping, I must've looked like crap, but he was worried about me! He said, 'I'm worried about you. You look like shit. You're working too hard.' I said, 'I've got to work.' He said, 'I'm fine. Don't worry about me.'"

"How did you take that?" I ask.

Nick makes a sound like he's been punched in the stomach. "That was a hard one. The whole thing was hard."

I ask what it was like for him to hear his client express concern about him.

"I was sort of disappointed in myself that it got to a point that he had to worry about me. But, you know, when he said he'd be all right, I think he—we had talked about it, and he was in as good a place as I guess you can get. He definitely didn't want to die. But I think he—yeah, you know, I think that's it," Nick says, realizing what he knows as he says it aloud. "He was better, I guess, at it than me. He stood up, and even though he was the one being executed, he wasn't haggard and a wreck; he was strong for his family—and for me, I guess. It made me feel sort of good for him and [to myself] sort of like, you need to step it up a little bit."

"What would that be?" I wonder aloud. "Step it up how?"

"You need to be the person that's strong for others."

"Is that what you were thinking when you said you were disappointed in yourself?"

"Yes. He doesn't need to be wasting any energy worrying about me." As we continue to talk and as Nick generalizes from this one experience to formulate an assessment of how he wants to be in relation to any client facing execution, he adds,

"I know I'm going to be affected emotionally, but I don't believe I should show that to them. I feel like I become a burden rather than—I mean, I'm going to be upset after every execution, that's a given, but—"

As I listen to Nick, part of me is wondering whether it wouldn't sometimes be gratifying for a client to see that he meant enough to his attorney that his loss would affect that attorney emotionally. Maybe in that sense an attorney's tears, even his "looking like shit," would be a gift rather than a burden. At the same time, I can certainly see why Nick, like others who expressed a version of this thought, would feel that it was wrong to position himself as the one in need of comfort when he's not the one about to be killed.

Sebastian remembers a client who would always ask, "How are you? How are you holding up?" after Sebastian had delivered bad news about the latest court ruling. "I remember literally being choked up with tears in my eyes," Sebastian says, so taken aback that the client "knew the toll that this was taking on me" and made a point of asking about it. "It made me want to work that much harder," he explains, "because it just reinforced the humanity [I was] dealing with." But he also felt as if he couldn't answer the question with total honesty; he felt obligated to favor reassurance over full disclosure. "I'd say, Oh, I'm doing fine. I'm a little disappointed, but I'm hanging in there. We've just got to keep the fight up."

They may not want to burden clients with their own sadness, but in the privacy of their own minds, they don't quite pretend to be unaffected. "I know how I'm going to feel," says Nick, having been through the experience of losing clients to execution several times. He has a ritual of sitting with colleagues when any client's execution is taking place, "waiting for the inevitable and drinking beer and just, you know, everybody's together."

Everybody's together, but within that solidarity is also the solitary grief of the attorney who is closest to the case and who is on that last phone call with the client until the very final moments. "You're on the phone, and you hang up the phone and usually come out all red-eyed," Nick explains. "You come out and say, 'That's it.'"

I ask if he had been with this group of colleagues during the execution of the client he'd just mentioned, the one to whom he was so close and who had worried about Nick's own health. "No," he answers immediately.

"I stayed by myself," he tells me. He had just described a scene of camaraderie, but he opted out of that shared experience when the grief was especially acute.

I ask why he chose solitude that time.

"It was just too—"

He makes a hand gesture that I read as "too much"—too intense, too much feeling. Precious as the group experience is, there is also a private grief that cannot or asks not to be shared.

Sometimes the solitude seems less a choice than a perceived incapacity. Simon tells vividly of the fragility and separateness he felt coming home from witnessing a client's execution. An old friend was unexpectedly in town, and Simon was on his way to see her when, getting out of the car, he "just lost it and said, I don't think I can do this. I remember the feeling was like—I'm sure it's a lot like soldiers coming home from war, or whatever. It was just like, I can't relate to anybody. I don't think I can go in there and be around anybody. I was really unsure, and feeling dissociated from reality, to some extent."

The prospect of seeing even a close friend felt impossible. And for a while afterward, Simon remembers "having flashback experiences, being really weepy, unable to hold it together." There is a sense in which, having worked so hard to "hold it together" in the period leading up to the execution, they then yield to the *inability*—sometimes whether they want to or not.

But the feeling of alienation in Simon's story is also striking. Though nothing outwardly marked him, Simon keenly felt that he "couldn't be around anybody." Having witnessed something that few people see, and having been affected in ways he could hardly articulate, what he was most aware of in that immediate aftermath was how unmoored and disconnected he felt.

Pamela has a story that illustrates the same thing from a different angle. It was the night of a client's execution. Pamela's mother's birthday was approaching, and in the overwhelming period leading up to the execution, Pamela hadn't taken the time to get her a gift, so that evening, she went to the mall. It felt strange and alienating to walk through the stores with the feeling that "I know they're killing this guy and you don't," she says. Finding herself in a gift shop that happened to have a couch in it, Pamela sank down onto it and then felt as if she couldn't get up.

"I sat there for an hour and a half," she recalls, "just watching people and thinking, You don't know. You don't know."

It's a striking scene: Pamela sitting among the crowds of people, her mind full of what she wanted to tell them but unable actually to say it aloud. "People would've thought I was crazy," Pamela says to me with a laugh. She knew she couldn't actually stand up and decry what was occurring in a world far removed from the shopping mall. But the scene is seared into her memory.

> I can remember it like I'm sitting on that couch right now as I'm thinking about it. It's one of those moments in life where you go, What you don't know is that right now there's a man, and they're tying him up in a room—you know, the way I was describing it in my head was, If I told you this, you would think, "We need to call somebody to stop this!"—There is a person being murdered, and we could fucking stop it, but we're not. That's the craziness, isn't it?

I ask Pamela what kept her sitting there on that couch all that time, not moving.

"Probably just exhaustion. I don't know. I was just sort of sitting there going through it all. Nobody spoke to me."

"You were having a dialogue with the public, but it was in your head."

"It was all in my head!" She laughs. "But I remember going through it fact by fact, just graphically going through it, what I want you to know, and if I told you, you would be horrified, and you would say, 'Who can we call?' "

I'm struck by the idea that Pamela's impulse was to declare an emergency, to mobilize others to intervene, even as she was immobilized by exhaustion and sadness. I ask how long she stayed sitting there.

"I was watching my watch and then: it was done. Yeah, I stayed until the execution happened. I sat through the execution on the couch."

Earlier Pamela talked, as others did, about the fear involved in having to make a last phone call or visit to a client. There's that immediate fear, and then there's also a persistent or cumulative sense of threat—the train barreling toward you—that affects attorneys in various ways.

"The emotional experience of seeing [clients] threatened is just like seeing anybody else you care for threatened," says Julian. "So the fear is for their life, which is in jeopardy. It's an ongoing thing; it's an undercurrent that's with you all the time."

That feeling sometimes makes its way into Julian's dreams. Whereas Paul describes recurrent nightmares in which he's trying to get to court and cannot, Julian's most persistent image is of being confined and unable to get out.

"I'll wake up in the morning, and I'll have a moment of panic and imagine myself trying to bust through the closed door of the bedroom," is how Julian describes it. That feeling, he suspects, derives partly from the claustrophobia of trying to fight within an unfair system and partly from the actual experience of visiting with clients on death row.

"You know, when you visit the client, they're in a small, enclosed space. They live in a small, enclosed space, and I think there's a certain amount of identification there, where I feel like I'm in the same situation. That's a constant thing for me."

Benjamin talks about both kinds of dreams. He has anxiety dreams similar to the ones Paul describes, dreams about "failing [his] clients" by learning at the last minute that the court has no record of something he thought he had filed, or by suddenly realizing that he has brought the wrong notebook to court and can't make his argument. And he has dreams that echo Julian's panicked feelings of confinement, nightmares in which he himself is a prisoner on death row. Benjamin explains,

> In the dream, it's ordinary. I don't remember dreaming about what I did to get [to death row], and it's not like, I'm innocent! Why am I here? Let me out! It's just: I'm there, and I'm awaiting the certainty of this fate with these other people who are all awaiting the same fate, and it's this sense of despair, that you're alone, and you're going to die essentially alone. . . . There's a very profound feeling of being by yourself, full of dread.

I wonder aloud about what in his working life mirrors that feeling. He's diffident at first, not immediately citing anything, but then he says,

> I have some cases in which I'm part of teams of people and feel a sense of support, and I have other cases where I really am the only person handling them. And, you know, if anything gets done on those cases, it's going to be done by me. And I often feel—I feel like it must feel to be hanging on to a life raft and have a lot of people trying to climb over you and onto the raft. And I hate feeling that way.

We talk some more about the image of the life raft. The people trying to climb on board, he says, are (in his emotional experience) all the people begging for his help: clients' families and the prisoners who write to him imploring him to take their cases. He says quietly,

> I just feel responsible for all these people. It's hard not to. I got into this because of a global sense of wanting to save people, and that

makes it really hard to say to the guy who's calling you in tears wanting you to help his son, I'm sorry, but I can't take on your son's case. . . . I'm already juggling too many things, and yet there is so much need. There's so many people saying *help, help, help.* . . . That is the thing that I'm haunted by: the people I cannot help, and the people that I feel guilty for not being able to help, even though rationally I totally understand, you can't do all these cases.

Later in the interview, Benjamin is talking, as so many of the attorneys do, about the delicate balance involved in trying to offer clients a mixture of hope and realism.

"I believe, rightly or wrongly, that the experience of living with some degree of hope has to be superior to the experience of living with despair and dread," he explains. "So if I can give the client some plausible reason not to give up hope, I would rather do that."

"You give them hope," I repeat. "So I'm wondering, do *you* get the despair and dread?"

"Absolutely," he answers. "There's a pile of despair and dread that somebody has to walk away from that conversation with, and I generally carry it back with me rather than leaving it with the client, to the extent that I can. I feel like in some sense I owe it to them. I live in the free world, and I have many pleasures that my life can give me to try to balance out the dread and despair. They have nothing. It's easier for me to bear it out here than for them to bear it in there."

And bear it he does. But as he speaks, the dream that he has described, with its image of profound and solitary dread, is vivid in my mind.

Pamela's graphic nightmares are frequent, and she recounts them with such amusement that it takes me a minute to imagine my way past the humor and into how frightening the dreams must actually be while they're occurring.

"I dream in red, I dream in blood, I dream in cut-up body parts," she tells me. She can't remember ever having had an execution dream, specifically. In the dreams, *she's* the one being threatened; she's the one in peril.

"I've had some where I've had to get up and walk around because I can't go back into this dream; it's too horrific. I had one once where I was being attacked, and when I woke up, [my husband] walked in, and I couldn't recognize him." At other disorienting moments in the night, Pamela remembers looking over at her husband and thinking, "That's not him. He's been killed, and the murderer is in my bed. And I'd have to touch him [to reassure myself], and then I'd go back to sleep." These experiences were especially intense for Pamela when she was working in a capital defense office that felt under siege, with a cascade of execution warrants and fellow attorneys who were so exhausted and demoralized that they "looked like ghosts. You're looking at them going, Wow. This is just destroying people."

In her interview, Pamela refers several times to compartmentalizing, not dwelling in waking life on the feeling of impending disaster. But she acknowledges that the feeling surfaces in dreams or in these moments of nighttime fear and disorientation.

"That's where it comes out," she says. "You know, I can be fine [in waking life]. You'll never know it watching me, but it's there. It has to go somewhere! But I don't *mind* it, you know. It's kind of a good place for me to have it, because I can take it there." Pamela means that she can tolerate the terror in her dreams, and indeed she does talk about these experiences with interest and humor, even though they are also very clearly frightening.

Sometimes the fear takes over without warning. I find it notable that several attorneys describe having strong reactions when watching films that in some way depict an execution. Adam says he has to look away, or even get up and leave, when he comes to that point in a movie. But while Adam already knows that these scenes will be tough for him, and he tries to avoid them, others have stories of panic reactions that have taken them entirely by surprise.

Isabel was in the audience at a public screening of a documentary film that showed the death house—the part of a prison where inmates are housed right before executions. "Sitting watching it, I had a panic attack:

throat closing, couldn't breathe, heart pounding," she recalls. "I had to get up, go outside, get some air. I really thought I was going to pass out."

Julian tells a strikingly similar story. He was at a film that depicted an execution and showed the prisoner struggling, even panicking, as he lay on the gurney. "I realized later that I just lost it, watching that," Julian tells me. "After the movie I went up and talked to the filmmakers, and I felt incoherent. I was a little shaky, and [at the time] I wasn't picking up on the fact that it was from having watched that scene and [having] generalized that scene to all my clients."

I suspect that even (or maybe especially) in a crowd of anti–death penalty activists, few would guess that a capital defender would be the one in the audience so susceptible to this kind of reaction. Here are the toughest attorneys immersed in the grittiest realms of legal work, people who dare to look where others might turn away. But it's exactly this exposure that both toughens them and leaves them more vulnerable. For capital defenders, death house or execution scenes in movies are not just cinematic glimpses of a foreign world; they are all-too-vivid reminders of what they have taken in and now carry all the time.

Watching these kinds of films, or having any experience that evokes their visceral memories of death houses or executions, puts them right back into those moments. Paradoxically, they become overtaken by what they couldn't fully let themselves feel when the event itself was taking place. At that time, they worked to manage and contain how much the experience affected them; during these flashback moments, they can't help but feel the impact of what they've taken in.

As Julian says, he didn't immediately realize what was happening when he reacted so strongly to the scene in the film. But as he has become more familiar with this kind of occurrence, he has grown able to recognize it even as it is happening. One time Julian was at the prison visiting a client. On the way in, he happened to glance over to the area where inmates visit with their families just before an execution, and he "felt this lightning bolt that started in my feet and just went up my head. A spike of fear, or panic." He describes this with some amazement; the reaction was so powerful and so unexpected. "I just felt like crumpling," he says.

It seems a terribly unsafe place in which to have this kind of reaction; it's not as if Julian could turn to someone and explain what was happening or ask for a moment of respite.

"But I recognized it, and stood there, dealt with it, and then went on to visit my client."

I ask what "dealt with it" involved. How does one deal with such a feeling while it's occurring? He says that simply recognizing what was going on went a long way toward helping him cope with it. Whereas during the experience at the film, he didn't understand why he felt so incoherent and shaky, here he quickly understood what was happening and was able to "stand there and let it pass or settle."

Able as he was to deal with it, Julian's prison story nevertheless suggests something important about the cumulative effect of capital defense work. After lawyers have been doing it for a while, any painful experience is layered with memories of similar previous experiences. As Isabel puts it, at some point each final visit with a client comes to feel as if "you're not just experiencing that client; you're sort of reliving all the other ones."

Recounting for me the story of a particular client's execution, Lou declares, "I'll never get over that." Later he says, "All the executions I've been through have left lasting scars and profound sadness."

"I think we were all just fragile," is how Keith puts it when talking about a period during which he and his colleagues lost several clients in close succession. I think of his use of the word *fragile*, and then I think of Paul's reference to feeling *shaky*, and I'm struck again by the vulnerability, the sense of being thin-skinned, that comes through so keenly in these conversations, right alongside toughness and strength.

Paul says that when he reads anything—even an ordinary story in the daily newspaper—that somehow reveals human tenderness, he'll surprise himself by being moved to tears.

"It happens to me a lot," he says, "and I've come to think maybe there's some stuff in there that's built up over the years."

"Tenderness is what gets to you, not the lack of it," I observe.

"Yes. Whenever I see human beings sort of living tenderness in their lives, it touches me deeply."

"What is it about those stories, do you think?"

"I just feel so much for people," he says quietly. "Doing the work we do, we just get so involved in our clients' and their families' lives, and feeling how life has been for them. I think that's part of it. It conditions you to be so sensitive to human struggle, human failure, human loss, human aspirations. [Then if] you experience it in any other context, it's just overwhelming."

I speculate to Paul that maybe reading stories of compassion or tenderness is moving precisely because it brings to mind all the times he has seen their opposite.

"That may be," he nods thoughtfully. "That may well be. Maybe that's why it touches me so deeply. I just feel washed over when it happens. I don't expect it. I think I've become conditioned *not* to expect it."

Anger can also overtake these attorneys. Sometimes it's pervasive and general; sometimes it's directed at people who seem somehow to embody or represent an arbitrary and uncompassionate system. Paul says that early in his career, after clients were executed he used to experience "tremendous anger and feelings of hatred, wanting to kill people myself."

I ask if those feelings centered on specific people.

"Judges, prosecutors . . ." he responds. "Not the people [who work] at the prison. I've never—I don't see them as the killers." To Paul, the people actually carrying out the execution are not in a larger sense as responsible for it as those originally handing down the death sentence. From other attorneys I heard variations of this thought, and some did also express anger or at least bewilderment at the prison guards: How could they do what they did? What was it like for them to do it?

"I didn't get stuck with that," Paul says regarding his feelings of anger and revenge, "but I have felt those feelings."

I'm struck by the parallels between Paul's feelings and those of murder victims' family members. Some people assume that the family of a murder victim would want their loved one's killing avenged by an execution. They are therefore often surprised when family members who *oppose* the death penalty acknowledge that they, too, have felt anger and hatred and a sense of "wanting to kill people myself." It's a common assumption that anyone who opposes the death penalty—let alone actively works against it, as capital defenders do—does not experience such anger. But as Paul's comments demonstrate, that feeling can come, as unbidden as the feelings of panic, shakiness, and fragility. The question is not so much whether one feels anger as what one does with it.

Some attorneys acknowledge feeling anger that is hard to get past. Keith tells the story of a particularly vigorous clemency campaign he was involved in, one during which he was so confident that the governor would indeed commute the inmate's sentence to life in prison that he didn't really face the reality of the execution until a few hours before it took place. Years afterward, he still wrestles with anger at that governor. "I'm not the most vindictive person, but I actually have terrible feelings for [the governor]," he says. "There's something about that execution that I'll just never forgive. I'm just sort of stuck on it. I don't think of myself as petty and vengeful, but there's a part of me that won't let go and wishes [the governor] would feel something that approaches the hurt he's inflicted." Here Keith refers particularly to the pain that the execution continued to inflict on the client's surviving family members.

"I do think there is something that you carry with you from all of this work," Gabe says after we've been talking a while. "It's like a heaviness, I guess. I think it's the sadness and the anger, sort of a combination. The anger at the system, the frustration—I think that stays with you."

A complexity here is that in some respects the anger is useful. Just as several of the attorneys say that outrage is part of what initially fueled their desire to start doing capital defense and to work so hard at it, Gabe says, "If you didn't have that sense of moral outrage, you know [the feeling of], How could you execute this guy whose confession was tortured out of him?—That anger helps you get up and do the work again. But I also think it can make you, or makes *me*, sort of an angry person."

Gabe recalls a persistent anger that consumed him during the years when he and his colleagues were dealing with so many execution warrants that they had barely recovered from one client's execution when they got hit with another. "I'd get up in the morning angry, get in the shower angry—I could wake up on a glorious day and still feel that way," he remembers. After a while, that kind of unrelenting anger began to feel corrosive rather than invigorating.

Simon also has a sense that anger has affected him in some troubling ways. "I always thought of myself as an optimist," he says as he thinks back to his life before he became a capital defense attorney.

> And I definitely know that's not who I am now. I directly attribute it to just how much shit I've been exposed to, just the worst of humanity, and—some people might think, "Oh, all the things your clients have done?" That's not what I'm thinking about [as I say this]. Certainly I've been exposed to some horrible things in that regard, incomprehensible in their horror, but right now I'm thinking more of just really sort of mean-spirited, dishonest, conniving actors in the system—judges, other lawyers, whatever. . . . Even coming out of law school I didn't have this cynical view of, not just the legal system but of human beings and their motivations, and I think now I have that. It's definitely a damage that I know is directly related to [doing this work] and that I wish I could go back and undo.

These capital defenders have been affected by their work in so many ways that cannot easily be undone. They use words like "wounded," "damaged," and "scarred." Part of what I heard them speculate about and reflect on was a question of *how* wounded, or, more precisely, whether they were affected in ways that interfered with their ability to work. After telling his story of witnessing a client's execution and then feeling so unable to be around others that he broke down even at the prospect of a visit with an old friend, Simon goes on to say,

> I think part of me says, I'm glad I [witnessed the execution], it was the right thing to do, it was good for [the client]. And part of me says, You know, it really damaged me. But then [another] part of me says, No more than a lot of other things I've been exposed to. I don't think it's been any more traumatizing than—maybe it has, but I

think—it hasn't debilitated me in terms of being effective, being able to keep doing work; it hasn't driven me away from it, so. . . .

The implication in Simon's musing is that the bottom-line criterion by which to assess how one has been affected is to ask whether it's been possible to keep working, or working effectively. Meanwhile, some attorneys tell of occasions when work became harder or even flat-out impossible.

During the time period so many have referenced, when capital defenders were likely to face pending executions repeatedly and in close succession, Roger was working on a case that, as he describes it now, "really put me over the edge." He got involved when the execution date was only weeks away, but given the particulars of the case, Roger was convinced that it was going to be possible to stop that execution. It wasn't, and that was "just devastating," Roger recalls now, "because I didn't prepare myself to lose. It was just brutal, you know?"

Almost immediately, Roger had to come back to work and confront another death warrant and go through the process all over again. "I was exhausted, physically and mentally, and demoralized. Just having a hard time getting the energy up to go back to that next box of transcript, that next box of record. . . . That motivation just went away. I can't look at this anymore. I just don't want to pick up that box."

The relentlessness, the need to get back up and do this again and again and again, comes through so vividly in these stories. Even when they are not completely overtaken by an inability to work, attorneys who are struggling with the cumulative effects of what they've been exposed to can find themselves internally resisting the demands of a case.

"When I need to do some critical work on somebody's case, I find a million other things to do," Paul says. "When it gets down to *having* to produce, having to work, I do it. But it's like, it's gotten to a point where I have less ability to concentrate and get something done until I have so much stress about it that I do it. It seems like that's gotten worse over time."

"I wonder if there's any part of you thinking, could we not have to go through this again?" I say.

"It's probably that," he agrees, nodding. The work pulls him in, and even, as he said earlier, keeps him from settling in to the place of sadness. Furthermore, his commitment to not letting his clients down remains as strong as ever. Yet there is also this undertow pulling him in the opposite direction.

Even more frightening to an attorney are the times when resistance surfaces so powerfully that it overtakes other impulses and makes continued work actually, at that moment, impossible. Adam tells about how, after a grueling period of one execution following another, he tried to write the brief for his next case and found himself unable to begin.

"I started doing some research, getting ready to do the writing, but I couldn't do it. I spent a lot of time looking out the window."

"What happened when you tried to write?"

"I was easily distracted. I'd find other things to do."

In fact, Adam says, there were plenty of other things that he also legitimately needed to do, and so for a while he could hide from the fact that he was actually having what he now describes as a breakdown.

"I didn't even get [what was happening] until much later, in hindsight. Since all the other things I was doing were part of my job responsibility, I wasn't twiddling my thumbs."

"So you wouldn't have said at the time, 'I'm having a problem'? It was, 'I'm coping. I'm fine'?" I ask.

"Exactly. A deadline would come. I would file a motion for an extension; the court would grant that."

This went on for a while, until finally Adam had used up all available extensions, and he could no longer ignore the fact that this was a worse problem than simple procrastination. "What hits you in the head," he says, "is that you've got this real deadline, and you still can't do it."

He ended up asking others to help him write parts of the brief, realizing that he could no longer pretend he was going to be able to do it on his own.

It's extremely difficult for these attorneys to admit that they've hit this kind of wall and actually can't do what they are expected to do. Isabel remembers that for a long time, "I was invincible. I could have one client executed a month and I was fine. Well, after a while I wasn't fine. I just hit the wall."

It's the wall of incapacity: I can't do what I've been able to do up to now. "I remember the moment," Isabel says quietly. "I was sitting at my computer working, and then I was just paralyzed. I just can't do it."

Sometimes the incapacity comes when attorneys happen upon something that brings them back to, and even makes them feel as if they are reliving, the worst of their experiences with death row or executions. By the point in our interview when Laurel describes such an experience to me, she has already spoken vividly of the persistent effects of losing clients. "Deep inside, it seems to rip you apart," is how she puts it. "You feel it in your head, you feel it in your heart, you feel it in your gut."

While there is a way in which that pain is ever-present, specific encounters can catapult it unexpectedly to the foreground. Because Laurel had been a witness to executions that were carried out by means of lethal injection, she was asked to testify when the procedure came under legal review. Preparing for that testimony required her to re-read a lot of material associated with those former cases and, most acutely, to remember what it was like to witness the executions. She had to remember details like the look on the inmate's face during the execution and the movement of his body.

"It brought it all back, [as if I were] reliving it," Laurel tells me. Compounding the difficulty was the nature of the legal challenge: the claim was that inmates who are executed by means of lethal injection actually feel more pain than had previously been assumed. Laurel was torn between wanting to help with the legal challenge and not wanting to find out that in fact she had been witness to greater pain than she had realized at the time.

Laurel gave the testimony, and then one day about a year later, she was sitting at her desk and happened to get an email that said something about lethal injection.

"Out of the blue, I just—I was paralyzed. I couldn't do anything but cry," Laurel says, her voice almost a whisper. "I really could not do anything. I didn't know what to do. I really was paralyzed. Probably to an outside observer it's fascinating. But I mean, I really—I couldn't read, I couldn't go back to work. I didn't even feel like I could leave."

Laurel was surprised not only by the intensity of her reaction but also by its occurring so many months after her involvement with the lethal injection litigation. It taught her that the impact of her experiences lives continually inside her and can overtake her without warning.

Whether because they have had actual experiences of this kind of paralysis or because they fear that they might, some of the attorneys offer assessments of what they believe would be too much for them to handle. These reflections provide an interesting counterweight to their emphasis on doing whatever is necessary and being able to handle whatever the work throws at them.

Explaining his decision not to go to a client's funeral after witnessing the execution, Elliot says, "I just did not want to go—partially because I was trying to draw a line under how bad it felt. I just felt too bad to go to the funeral. I needed to put it behind me, carry on."

Of course, the experience is not behind him entirely, funeral attendance or no. It was clear from our conversation that it has stayed with him in several ways. But I can hear in Elliot's comment the struggle to keep the harmful effects of the work within manageable limits. The effort leads sometimes to very personal assessments of what would be too much.

Roger had chosen to witness a client's execution, and even though he had the reaction described earlier—numb, so distracted and disoriented the next morning that he kept burning the bagels he tried to toast, and beyond that a feeling of depression that lasted several weeks—Roger says he doesn't regret witnessing; for several reasons, it was what he had to do at the time. Yet when the question arose regarding another client, Roger decided not to witness again.

"I just said, I can't," he tells me. "That's sort of where I am now. There are so many mechanisms you need to guard and protect yourself, and I don't know what would happen [if I witnessed again]. I don't want to go back to being depressed."

Benjamin made a similar decision. Having witnessed one client's execution, he decided not to do it again. "My decision not to go again is a personal feeling," he explains. "I don't know how to describe it except to say I am too deeply saddened by watching them die. And I feel like that reduces my ability to keep doing the work I do."

I ask how long the deep sadness stayed with him.

"It stayed with me for months. And it would come on you unbidden, in the same way that all kinds of really bad trauma do, in that you wouldn't even be thinking about it, and suddenly it would intrude into your thoughts, and you couldn't get it out of your thoughts."

Some attorneys who do witness executions, even several times, nevertheless wonder about subjecting themselves to the lasting effects of doing so. Caroline says she often used to tell other attorneys who asked for her advice that "if they had any reservations about it, my advice was not to do it."

I ask why she gave that advice.

"I think—and this must be because of what [the experiences] did to me—I think it's really hard to get past it emotionally. I think it has a huge effect. It's hard."

Nick, who is so clear about wanting to be present for his clients emotionally, and who insists on going in to the office the morning after an execution rather than letting the state know it has gotten to him, is nevertheless immediate in his response when I ask him whether he has ever witnessed an execution.

"I don't want to see it," he says.

We talk about this for a while. I bring up his earlier insistence on demonstrating that he isn't beaten down. Would witnessing an execution be another way of showing "the state" that he can handle anything, a way of saying, "You didn't get to me"? Or does this feel different to him?

"Actually, that's probably the one flaw in my argument," he says. "I think if you want to show they didn't beat you down and you're going to come in and take the worst they're gonna give you—"

He trails off. I think about the image of capital defenders as fighters. Given Nick's earlier description of himself, I won't be surprised if he says, "I'm going to show up at the execution to be there for my client and to let the state know I can take it." Thus I am struck both by his honesty and his self-criticism when he says,

"But I'm just a chicken. I don't want to see it."

"I wonder if there's a thought about self-preservation in there," I say.

"Oh, definitely."

"I know some people say they don't want to witness because they're not sure they could then keep going."

"Yeah, I'm afraid of that. I'm not so sure *now*, I mean, I think I could—I don't know. I've often thought about it: would I be more pissed off [after witnessing]? Knowing me, I probably would be. But I just don't want to."

So Nick has had the internal dialogue. He can imagine an outrage that would fuel his motivation to continue working, but he also senses the risk that this experience would simply be too much.

"I've talked my way out of it a couple of times," Nick goes on, laughing a little. He says that he explains to clients that if he arrives at the prison as early as required to go through the witnessing process, he won't be able to do any of the last-minute legal work that might offer some chance of relief (and that could buttress Nick's sense of having done everything possible to try to prevent the execution).

"Which of course is true . . ." I say.

"Yeah, it's conveniently true!" Nick is a bit sheepish but also straightforward in acknowledging that in this instance he chooses self-protection over other considerations.

Lou, like Nick, says that over a long career he has deliberately chosen not to witness executions, fearing that it might be "the one thing that could put me over the edge." When I ask whether a client has ever specifically told Lou he wants him there at the execution, he says, "Thank God nobody has!" Knowing what a high priority Lou places on relationships with clients, I wonder what he would do, how he would resolve that tension, if he *were* ever asked directly. Would he use Nick's strategy and say that witnessing would make it harder to engage in last-minute litigation?

"[Being asked] would be very hard," Lou acknowledges. "I think I would try to find somebody else to do it, somebody who doesn't have to go back to work the next day and fight for somebody else. Somebody who doesn't have to keep doing this." Lou's criterion, like Simon's, is about whether he would then be able to keep going. Even though Simon speaks about having witnessed and Lou speaks about choosing not to, it's notable that their emphasis is the same.

There are experiences one can't avoid, though, if one is still doing the work. Having been seriously affected by a particular client's execution, Julian then faced the prospect of another's. This was not, as some of these other stories have been, a situation in which one execution date followed immediately on the heels of another. A period of years had elapsed between the previous execution and the prospect of this next one. Julian had just about exhausted all possible legal claims, and was within two days of his client's execution. Sitting in his office working on the last in a long series of briefs, Julian got a call telling him that the execution had been stayed.

What should have been an occasion of exuberant relief was instead an experience of profound disorientation. "I had asked myself several times whether I could survive another execution date," Julian tells me. He truly wondered if he would be able to get through it, and yet it had seemed as if he would have no choice. "I was expecting it to happen, and I was struggling to make it emotionally," he recalls.

Then came the phone call with the unexpected reprieve, and Julian was overcome. He had been so braced against this next intolerable experience, so afraid of "feeling everything [he] had felt" the first time it had happened, that he was utterly thrown by the news of the stay.

"I felt like *I* was dying," Julian bursts out as he recounts this story. It's a stunning window into his experience, both the acuteness of it and the paradox. "My client survived," Julian goes on, "but that numbness— everything hit just as if he'd been executed."

It's as if the emotional and physical responses that Julian had experienced at the previous execution had already been set in motion simply by the prospect of this next one, so inexorably that even the news of the stay couldn't stop that tidal wave. Julian muses,

My body I guess was geared up to do all that stuff again, and it just did it. I was numb, I was in a state of—yeah, just complete numbness. Unresponsive. I mean, I'm speaking in exaggeration, but I was very hard to be stimulated by what I needed to do next in the case. What's going on? My client survived! And I continued, probably still continue to this day, in some fear of an execution date being set again. Like, I couldn't believe it. Totally disoriented.

The effects of this strange and paradoxical response still linger. "I'm still dealing with trying to get past that really *good* event!" Julian observes with some amazement.

The impact remains, sometimes long past what the attorneys anticipate. Through the shakiness, the panic reactions, the numbness, and the disorientation, their bodies are saying that it is impossible to insulate oneself from the pain and sadness that this work engenders. It's impossible not to take it in and be changed by it—in ways that never entirely subside.

# CHAPTER 6

# Not Talking

"I HAVEN'T HAD these conversations before," Gabe says as we near the end of our interview. "I don't sit back and ask how has all of this affected me, or what was I thinking at the time. A lot of the time I think I just try not to think about it."

"Do you have a sense of avoiding it?" I ask him.

"I think so. Because I think if you sit down and meet a client for the first time and you're thinking about your critically painful farewell with the last guy, if you're looking across from this person and thinking, 'Is that where this is headed?' it's not particularly—I don't know. That probably says more about me than it does about the work itself."

"What does it say about you?"

"I don't like painful stuff?"

He offers this almost with embarrassment, as if the answer reveals something a little too illuminating. Maybe he's right that his reluctance to look squarely at the painful effects of his work points only to a personal aversion, but I don't think so. Too many of Gabe's colleagues are as new to "these conversations" as he is and just as tempted to avoid a full confrontation with the question of how they have been affected by their experiences as capital defenders.

If the reluctance does say something about Gabe, what it says is not separable from questions facing anyone doing this work, questions perhaps inherent in the work itself. There are reasons why this kind of emotional self-examination has not been common among capital defenders, and understanding that is a key part of understanding their experience.

Few people really *like* painful stuff. If we do engage in the process of talking or thinking about it, it's usually because we've come to feel that the costs of not doing so outweigh the risks. If capital defenders haven't engaged in these kinds of conversations up to now, I'd guess it's not because they're more averse to painful revelation or self-examination than anyone else but because they haven't been sure that, in their situation, the benefits exceed the risks.

One reason to hesitate about discussing their work with others is the fear that what they say will be misunderstood. "You don't feel like anybody else can possibly understand your experience who hasn't been through it," Paul says, while Simon puts it this way: "You just have to do so much to explain and bring someone into your world view. It's just too hard to capture and then communicate." Julian is even more blunt: "It's too much trouble to talk about stuff and to have to translate it."

Capital defenders do a lot of extremely difficult things. But talking about one's experience, and particularly one's emotional experience, to unsympathetic or even merely uncomprehending listeners is a kind of difficulty that I suspect feels more wearying than energizing. It emphasizes the distance between oneself and others. Eric says he doesn't talk at this emotional level with his parents because, "I think there's no way that they can really understand. I just think it would be strange to—I mean, I don't even know how I would start that conversation."

Sometimes not starting the conversation is a deliberate choice.

"With some people, it's that they wouldn't understand; they wouldn't sympathize," Caroline explains. "You would be sharing something very personal with someone who didn't understand."

"Has that ever happened to you?" I ask.

"No. I probably never get to that point. It's not something that I would risk, if I don't know [how the other person would respond]."

While Caroline self-protectively avoids talking with people she isn't reasonably sure will respond well, another reason that capital defenders sometimes hold back is a feeling that they ought to protect other people from what they have been exposed to. Gabe says that sometimes he catches himself realizing his mind is full of—for example—the grisly details of a crime scene that he has just read about in a trial transcript.

"You think, Jeez, this is really unpleasant stuff to be thinking about all the time," he says. "If you were a baker, I imagine you would be think-ing about baking all day, not about people being killed in horrible ways." After another moment he adds, "You asked how [the work has] changed me. I didn't carry all that around before, and now it's in me."

I'm struck by his use of the phrase "it's in me." It reminds me of Pamela's words about her initial reluctance to make that terribly difficult final phone call to a client about to be executed: "I don't want that in me."

"I think that's why I try not to dwell on it," Gabe continues. "I don't want to carry that around the house."

Of course, at some level he is carrying it, whether he talks about it with his family or not. That, in itself, can be a challenge and a source of worry for the attorneys. Thinking back on a particularly intense period in his life as a capital defender, Julian says, "I didn't share this stuff with the family, but I'm sure I brought home the same intensity that I had at the office but just put a lid on it. It's got to have seeped out in some way." Roger, similarly, says he worries about "forcing [my family] to deal with the tragedy and the sort of horrific things [that I deal with regularly]. My wife said something to me at dinner a few weeks ago—we were sitting around and talking about our days, and she looked at me and said, 'So, can you tell us anything about your day that won't traumatize or horrify us?'" Roger laughs in recognition as he retells this. "It's funny, but she was also serious," he says. "I'm spending my days [thinking about things that] to normal people are gruesome."

Maybe family members don't want to hear the gruesome details, or maybe they don't always take the death penalty as personally as these at-torneys do. The first time Laurel stood vigil outside a prison during an execution, she had been working in a capital defense office for only a few months. The man being killed was not her own client, but she had seen her colleagues working hard on his case, and she found the execution, even from that distance, "really disturbing." She remembers coming home from that middle-of-the-night experience to a husband who "couldn't really understand why I was so affected. He was just like, 'These things happen,' which I knew was a bad sign for our marriage if I was going to continue to do the work."

It's hard enough to be numb or preoccupied or grieving, and harder still to worry about how all of that is affecting one's family. Without a spouse who can at least recognize the impact of the work, the marriage—or the work itself—can seem unsustainable.

Whatever contributes to it, then, there is often a feeling that they cannot or should not talk about what is actually foremost in their minds. And even harder and less common than talking about the details of their work is talking about how they have been affected by that work. "Do we get into the deeper conversations analyzing how this might be affecting us?" Karen says, paraphrasing my question back to me. "No. There are kind of glancing sarcastic references to it."

If the people who can best understand are those who have been through it themselves, then talking with fellow capital defenders would seem an obvious solution. But as Karen's words begin to suggest, this is less common and more emotionally complicated than it might at first appear.

"It's not really part of the culture of capital defense lawyers," Isabel explains. "We're not trained to talk about the emotional aspect [of our work]."

Indeed they are not. Legal scholar Susan A. Bandes observes, "Legal training and practice emphasize a cognitive model based on thinking, or impersonal logical analysis, to the exclusion of feeling, or person-centered values. Those who hew to this model are, unsurprisingly, most likely to complete and do well in law school" ("Repression and Denial in Criminal Lawyering," *Buffalo Criminal Law Review* 9, no. 2 [February 2006]; UC Berkeley Public Law Research Paper No. 789764; NYLS Clinical Research Institute Paper No. 09/10 #16. *http://ssrn.com/abstract=789764*).

The attorneys I interviewed are obviously highly skilled in the cognitive realm; their work demands it, and their intellectual agility is manifest in even a few minutes of conversation with them. But these are also the attorneys who were drawn to engage in what might be considered the most emotionally challenging of practice areas. As we have seen, death penalty work, particularly as these attorneys go about it, requires immersion in and confrontation with enormous amounts of pain, loss, and the litany of other challenges that they have described here. Neither legal training nor its culture has yet taken this seriously into account.

"People talk about the stress or the feeling of being overwhelmed, the deadlines, but people don't talk about the feelings," says Gina. "Or maybe it's just me," she continues with a laugh, "but I just don't see that."

"Would you want to?" I ask.

"I don't know. I mean initially I wanted to, but now I'd feel a little hesitant, I think *because* it's not part of the culture. I don't know where it would go. In a way I feel like I've sort of adapted, but in a way I think it would probably be healthy [to talk with others]."

Like Gabe, Gina initially ponders whether the obstacle to talking openly is only her own reluctance, but she then begins to situate her personal feelings within the context of capital defense culture and her interest in adapting to that culture and wanting to succeed within it.

"You don't feel like anybody else can possibly understand your experience if they haven't been through it," Paul offers as an explanation for his customary reticence. Before I can ask whether that means he talks with other attorneys, he adds,

"And even the people who've been through it, most of us can't talk about it."

"Why do you think that is?"

"It's too intimate, I think," he says after a silence. "I mean, it—you really have to feel some trust and acceptance at a very, very deep level, at least I do, to talk like this."

I remark that even though other capital defenders have "been through it," maybe it somehow feels as though they haven't been through it in exactly the same way.

"It's so intimate and private and individualized an experience," Paul responds. "Even people I've worked with and just admire tremendously and love, we don't talk about this. We just don't."

He takes a deep breath and continues, "Maybe we don't because there's wariness about it just being too painful. I don't know what it is, but we don't. At least, I never have."

Paul is not talking about not respecting other capital defenders or feeling a lack of kinship on the basis of their similar work. Instead, he talks about admiration and even love. Over and over his colleagues echo this feeling, describing an unquestionable solidarity and common understanding but also a singularity of emotional experience and an axiomatic truth: We don't talk about it. We just don't.

"We certainly talk a lot about issues, strategies, but we don't talk about *this* so much," Simon tells me, and at this point in the interview, we both know what *this* refers to. Once the attorneys and I were in the relevant conversational territory, *this* never seemed to need precise identification. All I had to do was ask, "Do you talk about this with other capital defenders?" and the attorneys knew what I meant. This: the raw emotion. What they have taken in, and what it is like to carry it.

"You don't have enough time," Simon offers as his first thought about why capital defenders don't talk like this with each other. "You've got deadlines you're under. When you're talking with colleagues and hanging out, you're either doing some war-story telling, sort of a 'have a beer' release kind of thing, or it's discussing [specific cases]."

They're not in the habit of it, and other things often seem more pressing and immediate. But there's something in Simon's response, as in the response of so many of his colleagues, that suggests it's not only a matter of not having the time.

"What would happen if you did talk?" I ask.

"It feels a little uncomfortable," he responds, laughing in a way that shows me exactly that discomfort. "It would be uncomfortable for me to talk about this with other colleagues. It's almost like: you don't do *that*." Again, the declaration: this is not what capital defenders do. I wonder if it's just a tautology—they don't do it because they don't do it—or if it is possible that this culture has arisen, or persists, out of a kind of collective self-protection, a response to each individual attorney's discomfort and wariness. Maybe there is a kind of implicit agreement not to probe this painful material too closely.

"Now, why [we don't talk], I don't know, but you don't do that," Simon says frankly. He pauses. "Who the hell knows?" he asks with a laugh. "I'm not sure why. It's a good question: why is there reluctance?" I hear him engaging with the question now, taking it up not just rhetorically but really trying to examine it. He speaks slowly, feeling for his response as he articulates it.

"I think viscerally it would be, 'If you can't handle it, move on,' or—it's not done because it's a sign of weakness. I'm just trying to think, right now, what would keep me from talking to, say, any [other capital defender]? Part of it too is, look, we all know we've been through this, we all know what it's like, and burdening somebody else with this stuff, they're all over-burdened anyway. I don't know. It's hard to know."

It is hard to know, but I think Simon's tentative curiosity begins to get at some of what lies underneath the declarative "We don't do that." Under the policy statement is an uncertainty, perhaps even a wondering: Is it weakness to have been affected by witnessing a client's execution, or having a painful final phone call, or any of the experiences that leave them with the grief, the panicky feelings, the cumulative impact that we saw in the previous chapters? How will they be seen if they talk openly about this kind of thing?

Although Simon observes that "we all know what it's like," it's my impression that in fact they *don't* necessarily know that their colleagues have struggled in similar ways. The immense respect that they feel for one another can have, as a counterpart, the belief that their colleagues are less vulnerable to the emotional impact of the work or somehow have a better handle on it. "She didn't seem to be as affected as I was," or "I don't have the kind of calm that he has," says one attorney of another while I sit silently recalling comments from exactly that colleague describing profound distress, shakiness, self-doubt, and all the rest. Continually in the attorneys' references to others in the capital defense community I hear this paradoxical combination of solidarity and isolation.

Wondering how they will appear to others is, therefore, a big consideration. But they also wonder about the personal risks of self-examination. What will they themselves see if they look at the emotional impact question too directly? And—perhaps their most pressing question—what will such reflection do to their ability to keep working?

Simon continues, "[I think there's a] concern that if you talk about it too much you'll let your defenses down, and you'll lose it, your mojo. You'll become too affected to be effective—whatever fears one might have about letting your guard down, your walls of defenses down, the fear that you can't maintain composure and ability to keep going."

Defenses, after all, get erected for good reason. If attorneys become too affected to be effective, or if they already *are* more affected than they have acknowledged, what will be gained by examining all of this with more than "glancing sarcastic references," to use Karen's phrase? This is what Gabe is worrying about when, in his comments at the beginning of this chapter, he imagines sitting with one client and feeling acutely the pain of a previous client's loss. Would that incapacitate him or prevent him from working as hard as he can for the new client?

"People talk about being overwhelmed [with work], but not about the sadness," Gina says. "You sort of wonder whether it's—in order to keep doing this kind of work, you almost have to set aside those feelings a little bit."

And Laurel says it this way: "I think attorneys in the work generally, and I can understand why, feel like they can't dwell on it. You can't dwell on it. You have to move on, or else you will be paralyzed if you start dwelling on the pain. Because if you start thinking about the end, how can you represent the next client?"

This may be part of why it feels hard to admit that sometimes they *are* thinking about the end, even very early on in a case. Benjamin says that even at those early stages of work, he will catch himself thinking about the eventual possibility of an execution, but

> I've never asked that of other lawyers, whether they feel that, and maybe that's not something anyone could admit, because it's too defeatist. . . . I'd have a hard time asking other lawyers, "Hey, when I go for the first time to visit a client, I'm already thinking about the funeral. Is that the same with you guys?" I don't know if that would be taboo to talk about. Even if they do experience it that way, they might feel, "I can't say that in front of other people."

So fear and doubt feel taboo both because they might threaten one's ability to keep working and perhaps because, as Benjamin suggests, they might jeopardize one's image as an energetic, optimistic advocate.

I see all these as real questions and not merely excuses for the attorneys' ambivalence about opening up to themselves or to others. If the attorneys' deepest sense of themselves as capital defenders depends in large measure on their being able to fight as hard as possible for each client, then anything that might threaten that ability is a serious concern. If they need to "set aside" raw emotions or defend themselves against the grief, loss, fear, doubt, and guilt that often arise in the course of the work, that's what they will do.

What complicates the issue, however, is that it's not unequivocally clear that such definitive setting aside is necessary, or possible. It may not even be in their or their clients' best interests.

It's interesting to me that Simon phrases the worry in terms of whether he (and other attorneys) would "become too affected to be effective," as though letting their guard down enough to talk openly about their experience would actually *cause* them to become affected by that experience and thus risk their ability to keep going. This is of course possible, in the way that tearing apart a dam can unleash so much rushing water that it becomes impossible to remain standing in its wake.

But I wonder if the fear is less about *becoming* too affected and more about *acknowledging* the extent to which they already are affected. After all, not one of the veteran capital defenders quoted throughout these pages comes across as impervious to the emotional intensity of the work. On the contrary, they are profoundly affected in myriad ways. Realizing this, the question becomes something more like: What to make of this? What to do with it?

After Gabe speculates about the risks of having "these conversations," I ask him, "Are there costs to not having them?"

"I'm sure that there are," he answers readily. "I'm probably not the easiest person to get along with in some ways, though I think I'm better now than I was for a while."

He reminisces some more about the particularly intense period in his career when one death warrant followed another for months at a time: "We used to drink whatever happened—I guess to keep from feeling that extreme emotion, either way. We drank when we got a stay, we drank when we got bad news—" He trails off.

"Because if you felt it, then—what?" I ask.

"I don't know," he says, shaking his head.

I suspect that's part of what is at issue here: not knowing what it would be like to confront rather than avoid these feelings and questions or to talk about them with others.

One of the attorneys had just gone through a client's execution the week before our interview. I inwardly wince at the unfortunate timing and wonder how he will feel about doing the interview so soon after that experience. He speaks openly about many things, including the recent execution. As we wrap up our conversation he says, "You know, I was actually thinking, boy, I don't know whether this is a good thing or a bad thing [to do this interview] today—it's so raw, how am I going to go and talk about recovering from executions when it just happened a week ago? But I think it was ultimately a good thing. It's important to work it through."

I suspect many capital defenders wonder whether it would be "a good thing or a bad thing" to confront the pain of executions so directly. But it's interesting that this attorney reflects on the value of "working it through." As the attorneys take up the question of talking or not talking, I find that the declarative "We don't do that" isn't all I am hearing. A tentative counterpoint emerges as well, suggesting a feeling that talking openly might in fact be a good idea and even, at least on one level, something they want.

"I would guess there's probably something, a very deeply repressed need to tell our own story that we're just in denial about too, a little bit," Simon says speculatively. "There's something in me that wants to be heard—but there's definitely a lot of ambivalence." That desire—however ambivalent it might be—is, as Simon says, to be heard and recognized and, I think, to be less alone in the emotional experience and perhaps to deal more directly with how their work affects them.

"Probably it's something we all should talk about more than we do," Karen says. "I have a sense of, It's something I haven't dealt with, and I probably should." Like several others, Karen engages in her own dialogue with the question throughout our interview. Having described her own and others' disinclination to talk in this way, she goes on to speculate about the potential value of breaking that pattern by talking more than is customary and genuinely dealing with it—whatever exactly that might mean.

Gina offers a similar thought as she imagines the possibility of a more emotionally supportive capital defense culture. "I know that [the work] affects people," she says. "I had one colleague who got seriously depressed, and I see that in some people, and I think maybe we're not as supportive of each other as we could be."

Perhaps even closer to the bone than "should" or "could" is the feeling of actively *wanting* the relief that talking openly might deliver. Paul tells me that, in decades of working as a capital defender, he has "never sat down and spent this amount of time talking to anybody about this in this way."

I ask why he is doing it now.

"I just, I'd like to feel better," he says quietly. "And I don't know if I can."

With these simple words, this naked honesty, Paul gives voice to a desire to do something about what he carries inside him. Recalling the sadness he spoke of earlier and the stress he described feeling each morning upon waking, he continues, "So I probably feel like if I could somehow—maybe talking about it is a way of addressing it. I don't believe that I can get rid of it; it's a part of me. But I think that *not* talking about it in this way can't be good."

"There may be no other profession," writes Susan Bandes, "whose practitioners are required to deal with so much pain with so little support and guidance" (ibid.). Bandes is discussing criminal defense in general, not capital defense specifically, but the point applies as much here as anywhere—if not more so. It's not hard to understand why questions about "dealing with it" are such new ones, or why the attorneys are so unsure about possible answers. If they were to do something other than simply maintain the "we don't talk about it" stance, what might their options be?

What they *don't* want to do is "dwell on it," in the sense that Laurel means when she says, "You can't dwell on it, or you'll be paralyzed." Dwelling, as Laurel and several others use the term, suggests a fear of paying the kind of attention to one's own experience that would be excessive, unhealthy, even self-indulgent. If instead of mere "glancing references" they were to turn their gaze to this issue so fully and so persistently that they feel themselves to be wallowing, whining, and—most dangerously— less effective, then in their minds the risk would be too great.

But are those two extremes the only available options? I hear that question in Paul's comments, and in Karen's and Gabe's and many others.' Might it be possible to deal with it without dwelling on it?

One obvious question suggested by all these reflections is whether capital defenders should find a way to talk more openly with one another about how the work affects them. There's no single answer to this. For some, a feeling of camaraderie and implicit understanding is paramount, and it may be sufficient. Pamela, for example, says that sitting with colleagues while a client's execution is taking place provides a wordless comfort that goes a long way. "You guys get where I am, so I don't need to talk," is how she describes it. "I don't need to think these thoughts, because you're thinking them too."

Roger echoes this when he says, "What I find meaningful is hanging out with these folks who know what it's like and have been through it, and we all understand each other and get it."

"You get a lot out of knowing that they get it, without anyone having to say it or talk about it," I observe. He nods in agreement.

Roger feels that this kind of mutual understanding means that if an attorney were really suffering, colleagues would be able to tell.

"We know when someone's right and someone's not right," he says. "We've all lived it. We've all been there, so we know what the other is feeling."

"So if someone were, I don't know, really devastated, really not coping, you would see that?" I ask.

"Exactly. We would sort of encourage them or—just sort of be around, you know? Kind of like when someone loses a relative, it's not necessarily anything you do. You're there if they need you."

Others are less sure that this is all that is necessary. Camaraderie is tremendously valuable, they say, but is it enough to address what may need to be addressed? Some clearly believe it is not and wonder whether something more explicit might be needed—to detect serious problems but also to reduce the likelihood that serious problems develop in the first place.

"We're in the trenches together. We have such respect, such admiration," says Lou. "We're a strong community, but there's not an institutionalized, structured process for dealing with the pain and loss."

"Would that be a good thing?" I ask.

"I don't know. It's a good question."

Within the capital defense community, it seems that this is an open question, one that is just beginning to be taken up. Some of the attorneys I interviewed feel strongly that it would be a good idea for capital defenders to talk more openly with each other than they do now and to address the emotional and physical impact of their work more directly. Isabel recalls that when she was going through a particularly hard time after several clients' executions, she felt "a little pissed off that there was no mechanism for dealing with this. I'm convinced, looking back on it—we didn't deal with it. Nobody dealt with it. The culture was, I'm not allowed to show that I'm affected by it. It was a lot easier to just pretend it was OK."

Easier, perhaps, but—as Isabel recalls—also harder. Says Julian, "I think we as a community need to do more to support each other by recognizing the traumatic aspects of the work." He suggests that it could be helpful to set up some kind of network where attorneys could speak with one another "not just about the logistics of the case but about how we feel about it and all of that—process the emotional aspects of it. We're not trained to do that! Everybody's got their own methods of denial . . . we've become isolated little suffering units."

"Isolated little suffering units" suggests something quite different from "we're in the trenches together," yet there's a way in which both are true. It's not as if Julian has not felt the camaraderie that Pamela or Roger describe, nor as if Pamela and Roger don't feel their share of private grief. If some attorneys were more adamant about the need for making more help available, that may have been a matter of personal preference or a reaction to the way the traumatic aspects of the work have affected their own lives. Or perhaps it reflects the extent to which they have been able to imagine what "dealing with it" might look like.

Some initial and still formative attempts to address this issue have begun to emerge within the capital defense community. Several attorneys told me about a session at an annual capital defender conference that is frequently dedicated to this purpose: making a space for the attorneys to talk about their losses and the accompanying grief.

"You can sit with others and talk about how you're feeling. When I first [attended the conference], I was sort of unkind about it," Gabe recalls, saying that he was dismissive of the session and didn't go. Then one year, having just gone through a wave of client executions, he decided to try participating.

"I went there and found I couldn't talk about it. I felt overwhelmed by it."

"You went thinking you might talk, and then you found you couldn't?" I ask.

"Yeah. I was just like, This is too hard. I don't want to deal with it. Which probably should have been a sign that I needed to do it."

Karen speaks about attending a gathering of capital defense attorneys where a member of the clergy held a session encouraging the attorneys to talk about loss. The format included a spoken invitation for attorneys to call out the names of clients who had been executed. Karen had lost a client very recently, but she didn't want to call out that name. "I'm not interested in sharing that way, the public sharing," she explains to me.

It may be that this just isn't the right format, or it wasn't the right one for these two attorneys. But these stories suggest to me that the question isn't only one of format. To some extent format certainly matters, and considering the relative benefits of various formats is worthwhile. But I think the issue is more complicated and layered than this.

If they are wariest about exposing their vulnerability to other capital defenders, then sharing in this kind of group setting might actually be their least preferred way of attempting to deal with what they are experiencing. Even amidst the camaraderie, the stakes may feel highest when an attorney considers speaking openly to others who are engaged in the same work. As Simon's expression of fear that others might think, "If you can't handle it, move on" demonstrates, revealing that they are *not* always handling it may feel too risky. What if their colleagues see them as not able to carry out the work effectively? What if they are discovered to be less capable than everyone thought?

The stakes may also feel high because of the amount of collective un-addressed pain that is present in a roomful of capital defenders attempting to talk in this way. As a reason not to talk about his emotional experience with his colleagues, Simon also cites not wanting to burden others who are burdened enough as it is. The other side of "I don't have to think these thoughts because you're thinking them too" may be, "I don't want to ask you to take on my struggles on top of your own."

"Maybe I'm projecting," Benjamin says, "but I feel like everyone else is probably just as sad as I am and just as guilty, so I don't want to make anybody uncomfortable by saying, 'I really need to unburden myself to you,' because I would be feeling like, I don't want to call you out on that."

It's interesting to me that although Benjamin speculates that other attorneys probably feel as he does, that commonality makes him less, rather than more, inclined to confide in them. He continues,

"I don't want to say, 'Let's share our badness of feeling,' because I've managed to keep it all—I've survived by keeping it all under wraps, and maybe I don't want to pull that off of somebody else and say, 'Let's look under here.' In case you're coping by doing what I'm doing. I don't want to take that away from you."

So interfering with a colleague's coping strategies is another concern. It's also possible that the cumulative weight of everyone's emotional struggle adds to the feeling of being overwhelmed that Gabe experienced at that conference session. A circle of people who have gone through the same thing is ostensibly a safer or more supportive space, but it may also be a space in which one's own emotions are intensified by the experience of seeing them in someone else. As vulnerable as attorneys feel talking about these things with people who *don't* get it, there may also be a very particular kind of vulnerability that comes with talking among people who *do* get it. The ubiquitous "support group" model is not necessarily the most comfortable model for everyone.

Whatever may be true in all this, Gabe's arriving at that conference session intending to participate and then choking when the actual time came tells us just how hard confronting this stuff can be, as well as how much attorneys may need to sort out before and during the process. My guess is that attorneys would need to choose individually—or would need help figuring out—their own ways of approaching this challenge.

"Everyone deals with loss in their own way," Nick says. "If you've got to deal with loss by going to therapy, or whatever, OK, but it's individual."

Only a couple of the attorneys I interviewed have worked with psychotherapists specifically for help with the effects of their work as capital defenders. Here, too, they feel the burden of having to explain themselves and their unique context. Says one, "All of this is new to [therapists].

People are so fascinated by the whole execution thing. It's like, 'I've never had a client say *this* before.' So you have to spend a lot of time explaining."

And another:

> You have to explain a heck of a lot . . . I think some therapists probably can't get past their own biases, maybe because they've worked so much with persons who were victims of violence or sexual offenses. This is just an intuition I have from talking with some of them—they don't have a natural sympathy for the perpetrators so don't have an immediate sympathy for persons who are traumatized because they're trying to protect the perpetrators. So there's a hurdle there that some therapists may have to get over.

There's a worry, then, that mental health professionals will have the same biases as other people and that their prejudices about criminal defendants will leave them unsympathetic to the suffering of the attorneys who defend them. When attorneys who seek therapeutic help encounter this lack of sympathy or the wide-eyed curiosity of a therapist "fascinated by the whole execution thing," it can feel as though they are being asked to explain and even justify an entire social policy instead of getting recognition for their distinct personal needs and experiences.

It seems plausible that some psychotherapists may have difficulty getting past their own biases, as the attorney above suggests. But the opposite could also be true. As a result of their training and personal inclinations, mental health professionals might have a more multi-dimensional understanding of the factors that could lead an individual to end up on death row, and a feel for the complexities of any human story. Many therapists must sympathize and even identify with an attorney's drive to save a client and the particular pain that comes when that effort fails. So a capital defense attorney in a psychotherapist's office might have cause to feel especially wary or, on the other hand, especially understood. It's a gamble, as talking to anyone about their experience inevitably is.

Those attorneys who have tried talking about their experience with psychotherapists generally seem to agree that "talking about it helps,"

as one puts it. Another mentions that the relaxation techniques a therapist taught him have been useful during the day-to-day pressures of his
work life.

Only one describes seeing a therapist who specialized specifically in
trauma and who could, on that basis, apply a general understanding of
trauma to capital defenders' experiences. But seeing capital defenders'
panic reactions, numbness, or abiding sadness and shakiness as symptoms
of trauma is in itself a very new idea. Over the past two decades, recognition of trauma has grown tremendously, deepening capital defenders'
understanding not only of their clients but also of their clients' families
and the families of murder victims. The new frontier is for capital defenders to extend this understanding to themselves by including their own
symptoms and experiences within the definition of *traumatic*—and for
mental health professionals to do so as well.

If having a variety of available options would allow attorneys to choose
what might work best for them personally, to what extent should the capital defense community be responsible for providing those options? Some
attorneys, as we've seen, feel strongly that the community ought to take
more responsibility for helping its members. Speaking more specifically,
Adam speculates that "there probably should be some sort of acute trauma
team, maybe put together by [the defense community], where you'd have
mental health professionals [and] other lawyers who have been through it,
and they'd go to a state where there's been an execution and meet with the
folks who have worked on the case."

I ask Adam what he imagines this team might do. Would it be about
creating an opportunity for attorneys to speak all together in a group? "I
think people want to find a place where they can vent this stuff," he says,
"but there could be one-on-one [opportunities] too. Each person could
choose what they felt comfortable with."

Laurel agrees both about the need to offer more help and about the
value of offering a choice—group or one-on-one. "Having a counselor
who specializes in trauma on call—I think that would be ideal," she says.

"Would you require people to see the counselor or just make the option available?" I ask, trying to get a clearer picture of what she might be envisioning.

"It's funny," she replies. "My gut is I would not require it, but then again, I'm thinking, they do require it in police work and other kinds of work where [people have] gone through something traumatic."

We both pause to consider that.

"Why was your gut saying *not* to require it?" I ask.

"Because I know how resistant lawyers are to it!" she laughs.

"I wonder if that's a reason *to* require it," I say, joining in the laughter. But as I think about it more, I realize that Laurel's analogy to police work has interesting implications. When a profession requires—just goes ahead and builds into its structure—that its members attend to the traumatic aspects of their work, or simply to the fact of its emotional impact, maybe that provides a collective recognition from which everyone implicitly benefits. Maybe each individual attorney would feel less exceptional, less likely to be viewed as "too affected," if the potential for being affected were routinely acknowledged. And maybe its being required would allow some attorneys to take advantage of the help in a way that feels more face-saving and less an admission of special need.

Even with all these persuasive arguments, I don't know that I myself would go so far as to argue for mandated counseling over offering a range of available options. But I think the advantages of collective acknowledgment, a community-wide recognition that "being affected" comes with the territory and is not an indication of inability or ineffectiveness, would serve all capital defenders, regardless of whether or not they choose to seek out additional help.

Sometimes it may take someone else's initiative to help attorneys feel that intentionally sharing their emotional experiences is valuable. When one of Keith's colleagues urged some local capital defenders to come together for such a gathering, Keith's first thought was to agree simply because his colleague had asked.

"I think when I recognized it in someone else, the sort of counselor part of me said, OK, I can engage in that because it will be helpful to [my colleague]," he says.

"Because *she's* hurting," I say.

"Right, because she's hurting. But once you get into the process, your [own] emotions come up."

Keith ultimately felt grateful that his colleague had initiated the process. "I think it was her effort that helped us appreciate just how much we were all hurting from these losses," he says. "She helped us to see that we had obligations to each other. You had these walking wounded all around. There was just no—we hadn't developed any sort of traditions or routines about talking about it. Some people would get drunk. I never really did that—"

"What had you been doing to deal with the losses?"

"Nothing! Not dealing with it."

So he went along with his colleague's suggestion that they all make a point of talking with each other more openly. He says that "it was a deeply emotional experience" to share in that way. "Sometimes it was like, OK, do we really have to talk about this? . . . But I think we all sort of felt a need to make sure that we were taking some care of ourselves."

Taking care of each other, taking care of ourselves. So many things can be true in different and overlapping ways. They don't want to burden each other, but doing something for a colleague can be an easier entry point than doing it for oneself. They don't want to seem self-indulgent or to overstate their own role in the death penalty story, yet at the intimate center of their analysis of the question "to talk or not to talk" can be a heartfelt expression of their personal desire to—as Paul puts it—simply *feel better*.

What does it mean to be affected by one's work as a capital defender? What does it mean to admit it? I think back to some of the attorneys' stories of showing up at work the day after a client's execution so the state won't see that it has gotten to them. I wonder now how the whole idea of being "gotten to" figures into this question about acknowledging or revealing that one has been affected. If you are affected, if the work has gotten to you emotionally or physically, does that mean you've lost the battle? Framed that way, it would give attorneys another reason to avoid acknowledging how badly they might actually be hurting. As Isabel says, it would be easier to "just pretend it was OK."

Caroline explains in rather moving detail the ways in which capital defense work engenders compassion toward other people, flawed and weak though they often are. She talks about coming to know so much about her clients and their lives that she cannot help but see them as human beings and not judge them. As she talks, she uses the phrase "human frailties" a few times, so I ask, "Do you extend that compassion and acceptance of frailty to yourself as well?"

"Probably not as much as I'd like to," she responds. I would guess that many people—capital defenders or not—would tend to respond that way. It *is* often harder to extend compassion to ourselves. But I wonder what might happen if capital defenders were able to do this to a greater degree.

What if frailty—vulnerability to being affected by one's experience— were seen not as an exceptional trait, but as a universal one? What if having an emotional and physical reaction to the responsibility of trying to prevent a client's death, or to a wrenching last prison visit, or to witnessing an execution, were understood as common? What if, instead, impervious-ness were considered unusual?

While discussing the talk-or-not-talk dilemma among capital defend-ers, Julian says, "There's a resistance to sending any perception that you might be weak, you might be vulnerable—that you're human, you know?" Maybe, Julian is suggesting, this is not about incapacity but about com-mon humanity—exactly what capital defenders work so hard to recognize and to advocate for in their clients. Maybe being emotionally and physi-cally affected by one's experience as a capital defender is the unsurprising consequence of being a human being placed in this particular crucible, exposed to its particular sorrows and demands.

# CHAPTER 7

# The Victories

AFTER HE'D BEEN a capital defense attorney for several years, Gabe agreed to help a relative who needed a lawyer for a traffic court hearing. He was amazed at how easy it was—not just the work itself but winning the case.

"I thought, Wow, this must be what it feels like to do this kind of law on a daily basis," Gabe says, laughing. "That's what I had always thought a lawyer would do: You get a case; you fix it. You get clients the result they want."

There are, in fact, areas of legal practice in which attorneys win more often than they lose. Post-conviction capital defenders can become so accustomed to operating within a framework where, as Karen puts it in Chapter 3, "it's the norm to lose," that they are sometimes startled into remembering just how atypical that framework is. Winning so easily, Gabe says, was "weird but satisfying."

Tellingly, though, the experience did not make him want to change his practice. "The last thing I want to do is spend my days talking about people running stop signs," he says, and I am reminded of all the reasons he and others have given about why they chose capital defense in the first place. It doesn't surprise me that dealing with traffic violations is neither interesting nor high-stakes enough to satisfy Gabe over the long term.

Still, I wanted to hear more about how these capital defenders define success. Do they define it in ways that mean they seldom achieve it, or do they understand the term in such a way that they are able to experience success more frequently?

The capital defenders I interviewed are widely recognized and highly regarded within their field. They are invited to speak at conferences and to consult on others' cases. Several have won awards and honors and have worked on cases that received considerable attention from both the courts and the media. Arguably, they are clearly successful in a professional sense. But this kind of success, however gratifying it might be, is not at the heart of a capital defender's assessment of what constitutes victory or achievement in the work itself. It was this core inquiry that I wanted to consider.

When you do win, in capital defense, you win in the biggest possible way: you save an individual from execution.

"I had one case where the client actually got off death row," Gina tells me. "I got to call the family and say we won, and they were so appreciative. In that particular case, I did save a life."

"What was the impact of that on you?" I ask.

"I think for me, it's kind of the fuel. Even before we got relief in that one case, I knew that relief is a possibility, and I think that's what drives me."

It would be one thing if they knew at the start that they would never win. But even at the post-conviction stage, saving a client's life is not impossible; it's just extremely rare. As Gina says, it's that possibility, so slim but so powerful, that keeps defense attorneys in the game. And because they view themselves as trying to prevent an execution, they naturally see overturning a death sentence as the ultimate victory.

"Obviously, I like the ultimate winning," Roger says. "Getting them off death row is about as good as it gets. It doesn't get any better than that."

To overturn a death sentence and thereby save a life is a victory over many things, including the odds. But some attorneys acknowledge that only a capital defender would truly view a life sentence as a win. "Let's face it," Nick says. "Who thinks that sending somebody to jail for life without parole is a win? But we take it as a win."

Phrasing it as he does, Nick introduces a note that I hear repeatedly, in various ways: success is as much about how they take it, interpret it, and experience it as it is about any kind of objective measure. We've seen that, in the context of capital defenders' work as a whole, even a victory can be emotionally fraught. There is Julian's story of getting a last-minute stay for a client and yet reacting, internally, as if the execution had gone through. There is Simon's story of a big win that, while genuinely a story of victory, also revealed to him the extent to which he had internalized a sense of fault for previous losses. There is Benjamin's assessment of the randomness of winning and the resulting impossibility of interpreting victory as proof of skill or effort. It's tough to separate their experience of winning from their overall experience as capital defenders.

It's clear that the ultimate goal, and thus the ultimate victory, is to prevent an execution entirely. But so much of post-conviction work is about the steps along the way that may halt an execution at any given point. Attorneys may litigate late into the night and get a stay of execution at the last minute. The stay doesn't remove the threat of execution entirely; it just stops it from happening on this particular day so that the court can rule on whatever legal issue has been raised. But even if it only halts the train temporarily, in that moment a stay can feel like a triumph.

"Delaying an execution is a victory," says Karen, and others frequently agree. What makes a delay so valuable? Sometimes a delay can in fact make the ultimate success possible. "It was a wonderful thing when I got [one particular client] off death row," Adam remembers. "After a death sentence, new sentencing hearing, death sentence, new sentencing hearing, death sentence, new sentencing hearing, *finally*—I kept him alive long enough for the US Supreme Court to decide *Atkins*, so his mental retardation saved his life." Adam is referring to the court's 2002 decision that ruled the execution of intellectually disabled* individuals unconstitutional.

"I was very proud of the fact that I had three times in a row gotten

---

*"Mental retardation" was the term used in the Atkins decision. Since then, "intellectual disability" has become the preferred term legally and culturally.

him relief, which allowed him to stay alive long enough for the *Atkins* decision to come around," Adam continues, "because I know there were a lot of people who *were* executed who had mental retardation."

This is the legal equivalent of keeping a terminally ill patient alive long enough for a new treatment to become available. It's a long shot, but sometimes it works, and in the aftermath one can feel simultaneously proud and regretful about all those for whom the new treatment—or new legal ruling—came too late.

Many times, though, a delay turns out to be just a delay, not a step toward preventing the execution entirely. Yet among these capital defenders, a delay seems generally understood as a victory even on its own terms. "[Sometimes] you can't stop the train, but you can slow it down," Isabel says, implying that slowing the train is by definition something to strive for. Julian tells me that even when he feels the futility of trying to prevent an execution in a particular case he will still "jump in and try to do something to slow it down." He adds, "That's a habit you may have found with a lot of my colleagues—trying whenever we can to do something to slow things down."

He's right that it is common, and, I think, not only as a habit but also as a drive with multiple motivations. In Chapter 4, I quote Adam's comment that what a capital defender does is "make the state work like hell if it wants to take somebody's life." This is one motivation for trying to slow things down. "I do think there is some solace in, you made them work too," Adam goes on to say. "If you were up for three nights in a row, you know they were up three nights in a row over at the attorney general's office. You made it as hard as you could possibly make it for them to take the life of another human being. There *is* something about that [that is satisfying]."

Success, in this sense, means making the state work as hard as possible for *its* victory. While this rationale may make sense in the language of the legal fight, one might reasonably ask who benefits from it. How does slowing the train benefit the individual tied to the tracks and dreading its inevitable approach? It's easy to see that delaying an execution is beneficial when it ultimately leads to a client's exoneration or to overturning the death sentence, but it may be harder to see why prolonged time on death row is necessarily better for an individual who does eventually get executed.

Perhaps capital defenders—feeling, as we've seen, that clients' lives are in their hands—are simply disposed to believe that anything that prolongs life is by definition a victory. But in our exchanges, what also emerges is their interest and even investment in the quality of the lives they are fighting for.

"For me, that's what being a death penalty lawyer is about," says Isabel. "You can't [necessarily] save their life, but you can save their humanity." Like many of the interviewees, Isabel experienced a period when several of her clients were executed in close succession. "You take your victories where you can find them," she says as she reflects on that time. "[During that period] there was this group we couldn't save, but I guess it felt like we were helping them to die, helping them to find some dignity in those last days or weeks. . . . If nothing else, we could help them preserve their humanity, and maybe that was the victory."

Perhaps that in itself is not an argument for *prolonging* life, but once attorneys expand their definition of "victory" to include "helping clients preserve their humanity," all sorts of other possibilities may emerge. "You have to redefine a win," Nick says. "You take the positive things that happen: my client was executed, but in the last six months he finally connected with his son or his mother, and [I] helped facilitate that. Is that a win?" he asks, perhaps rhetorically. "There are positive aspects of even the worst thing."

Once again, Nick draws on his previous analogy between oncology and capital defense work: "It's like—your client is terminally ill, and you're going to try some experimental drugs, which could work; you're going to do whatever you can. It's, I'll keep you alive for as long as I can and try to give you a quality of life."

Clients will often ask their attorneys to help them in ways that are not explicitly legal: asking them to send reading material, for example, or to run interference when there's a problem with the prison administration.

"I'm happy to do [those kinds of things]," Nick says. "That's the quality of life thing. In a sense—when I talk to you now, I think maybe it's *because* I know that the situation is sort of almost hopeless. The deck is so stacked that they're probably going to be executed eventually, so it's almost hospice-like. You're trying to help people that you know are doomed, are terminal."

"While perhaps not quite having an overt acknowledgment of that?" I ask.

"Right. Because you *can* win cases at the last stage. I just won a case that I didn't expect to win. I fully expected that we'd be having an entirely different conversation about [that client] right now."

So there are surprises, as perhaps there are in oncology as well. Meanwhile, Nick's point about quality of life echoes what several others express and offers a possible response to the question of whether it's a kindness or a cruelty to delay the execution: it depends on what the client's life is like along the way. Clearly, helping to keep a client alive can also mean creating the possibility for other kinds of surprises. If the client is then executed, attorneys are left with a paradoxical feeling that Nick tries to convey when he says,

> Obviously the bad aspect of it is that you lost somebody, but that is—well, I don't want to say that it's outweighed, but there can be so much good that happens too. How many times does it happen that the family was estranged, and then you work and get them back together at the end, and over the last three or four months they've bonded again? You do good things that aren't apparent, that don't come out in the case report. You don't win the case, but you do good things *for* the client that probably wouldn't have happened otherwise.

Nick twice refers to reconciliation among previously estranged family members as a positive event—a kind of victory—that can happen for a client on death row. Others also give this example. When I ask Roger to say more about why he believes that "keeping them alive as long as possible" is a good thing, he replies, "There are so many cases where they reconcile with their family at the end. If they weren't alive all that time, they never would've had that chance." Similarly, Pamela describes these kinds of reunions by saying, "The child gets to live with a memory of her father that she wouldn't have had. That's a very big part of what we do that we have to hold on to. . . . We get to make the bridge and forge those bonds that sometimes hold."

The attorneys tend to characterize these reconciliations not only as positive happenings but also as positive events that the attorneys themselves help to make happen, or at least to make possible. Keith is explicit about this when he recalls a client who was executed for the murder of his wife. As part of the clemency campaign, Keith and the other attorneys reached out to the client's grown children, who had been estranged from their father over the many years that he sat on death row. The children eventually became outspoken opponents of their father's execution.

"He did a horrible thing in killing [his wife] and destroying his family," Keith says now, "and there is a sense that our post-conviction work salvaged his family, reconciled his family. . . . The flip side of the anger that I feel [about the execution] is I feel a real sense of satisfaction that we succeeded at bringing that family together."

Attorneys can therefore find success in, as Nick puts it, the good things they do for their clients that are not publicly apparent but are nevertheless meaningful. "There are cases that are so sad because the clients have been so abandoned, not just in their personal lives but by their lawyers," Karen says, "and you come in at the last minute, and they're just so grateful that somebody did *something* for them. And sometimes that's why you do it. You know there's no hope in doing it, but it means a lot to the client. And ironically, in that sense it feels like you did something meaningful for the client."

If, as often happens, a client on death row feels abandoned or betrayed by the lawyers who represented him earlier, a post-conviction attorney can come in at latter stages and at least try to provide a dedication and commitment that the client may not have experienced before. In these stories, the act of showing up and litigating for a client has value even apart from the outcome. Repeatedly, I hear the attorneys finding and articulating meaning—and even, in a sense, success—in terms that are not dependent on whether they ultimately win the case.

In addition to showing up for a client, another frequently cited way of viewing oneself as effective is in "giving voice" to clients. "There is something really soul-satisfying about that," Simon reflects. "There's something about—some poor hack who just never had a chance and probably tried to get some kind of voice early on, probably got ignored from the very beginning but had something to say, whether it was, 'Look at me' or 'I need some help' or whatever, and that probably got squelched pretty quickly, never got heard, and then he did something really terrible."

He pauses, and I think briefly about psychologists who interpret criminal behavior in just this way, as a garbled attempt at communication. Simon continues,

"There's something good about saying, 'You know what, the trial silenced you, the [trial] lawyer didn't do his job, the judge didn't want to hear, and by God, we're going to let you speak before you die.' "

"And you get to be the conduit of that, through what you write and what you file," I observe, noting once again that this is not just something an attorney like Simon can witness, but very specifically something that he can take pleasure in facilitating.

"Yes, absolutely, that's what I'm talking about," Simon agrees.

Connected with the idea of "giving voice" is the idea of making a record of what the client said and did or, even more pointedly, of what others may not have recognized or understood. The job of the attorney at this stage, Simon suggests, is to discover and then tell the truer or fuller story. Picking up on and repeating his own phrase "soul-satisfying," Simon goes on to say that

> it's soul-satisfying to set the record straight so that—let's take a
> habeas setting where the record did not get told properly at the trial
> so that all anybody knows about it is, "So-and-so is an animal, a
> monster." We all know, having done this work, that that's not the

truth, and it's just a matter of someone being willing to go out and, as it were, disprove it, find out what the real truth is. Going out and listening and finding out what really happened and making sure that that gets told before this person's taken off the planet, and hoping that might even stop it, but at least saying, Look, you can kill him if you want to, but it's not right and here's why.

Though good capital defense typically involves exactly this—getting the more complete story of an individual and presenting it in a way that might mitigate against execution—it is interesting that Simon seems to be suggesting that this effort is satisfying not only as a strategy but as an end in itself.

"There's something there for you that isn't just about mitigation," I speculate aloud. "You seem to be saying that even apart from the question of 'will it save him,' you want to get the story told."

Simon nods. "For some reason I keep thinking that some time, some day, this is all going to be made right. It may be a thousand years from now, but in order for it to be made right, we're going to have to tell them."

It is interesting to consider whom Simon imagines telling. "And so you need the record," I say, joining into the story.

"Right, you need the record," Simon repeats. "Now, that's a lawyerly way of seeing the world, but—you've got to make a record so when the tabulations are made up there at the gates, that person's not going to get thrown over here because you have been able to say, This is not the whole story here, St. Peter; it's a whole 'nother thing here."

A lawyer makes a record. Others echo this thought, as when Gabe says, "Sometimes what you're doing is just bearing witness or making a public record of some injustice that you know you're not going to be able to correct because there are so many layers of technicalities that block you from getting the case considered on the merits."

You focus on making a record when that feels as if it's all you can do, Gabe is saying, but, again, there is a sense that making that record also has its own urgency and its own justification. Caroline puts it this way:

If all else fails, what you're doing is making a record for the future.
When I see something that I think is particularly egregious, just
a real injustice that upsets me because it is so wrong, I feel like
it needs to be made known, and that making it known is an
accomplishment. Hopefully you can correct it and change it, but if
you can do nothing else, you can expose it, and to me that has huge
value. That keeps me going no matter what. That may be, as much
as anything else, although I'm sure it's not the only thing, what has
kept me doing [this work].

Making something known is in itself an accomplishment, just as giving voice or showing up for a client can feel like victories in themselves.
Yet it has to be said as well that while the satisfaction of these kinds of
victories may be genuine, it is not unalloyed.

"You think sometimes, well, we managed to get the real story out, or
gave the client a voice that he never had before," says Roger in response
to my question about what counts as success in his mind. "I mean, that's
success in some ways. In some cases it's important to the client to feel that
he's been advocated for, but—you know, I don't classify that as a big success because that's what we're going to do for everybody."

Roger sees these actions as so basic to his way of working that he
doesn't quite feel he can count them as triumphs. Meanwhile, the ultimate
loss is never far from their minds. Says Adam, "In any endeavor, in order
for there to be success, you have to do both what is necessary and what is
sufficient. Doing everything you can when your client nevertheless dies is
necessary, but it's not sufficient. It's not much solace, in fact."

That insufficiency, as we've seen, haunts the attorneys no matter how
they may manage to offset it. Awareness of insufficiency is probably an intrinsic part of the experience. Just as others have suggested, Karen says that
there are "non-legal ways" to measure success in capital defense work. But,
she goes on to say, those ways are "so intangible, and it's very hard to say,
Well, that client felt better because somebody advocated for him, while the
little voice [inside you] is going, But he was executed! But it's often how we
console ourselves, or what we say to each other," Karen acknowledges. "We

say, 'You told the story'—for some great book of history that we think we're telling the story for!"

All these comments about "making a record" have, as Karen implies here, an element of belief in some future audience who will pay attention. She continues, "We say, You moved the dialogue forward; you made the client feel like somebody was fighting for him."

"But I hear that that doesn't really do it for you," I remark, responding to her tone more than her words.

"None of it does."

On some level, none of it does. None of these successes or satisfactions entirely offsets the impact of the loss. But as we have seen, so much of what the internal struggle is reduced to in the end is a question of who these capital defenders want to be, what role they want to have played. Elliot remarks, "Sometimes you'll say, Well, even if I'm not doing any good here, at least I'm trying to stop something bad." and his comment is about where he stands not just in the capital punishment landscape, but perhaps in the broader social landscape as well.

Elliot then brings up Albert Camus' novel *The Plague*.

> There's this point in the book at which [the main character] says
> he's a man who has decided to have no further truck with injustice.
> I identify a lot with that. I use that to inspire myself. At some point
> I can say, Maybe I'm not doing the right thing or something that's
> good, but I'm not aligning myself with injustice. I'm defining myself
> in opposition to it. Some days that's all you have. Some days you
> have a lot more, but some days that's all you have.

Whether this feels like a lot or a little probably depends on the day. What I see, though, is the way in which these attorneys are able to find or create meaning for themselves while working to align their efforts with their sense of identity.

"That's a hard question," Gina says with a laugh when I ask her what defines success in capital defense work. After a moment she responds, "I think for me it's knowing that I did my absolute best. I mean, clearly, of course, I want to win every case, but—I feel like my conscience is clear if I do the best I can, and then that's all I can do."

I ask about the opposite. If one applies those terms, what constitutes failure?

"There's always that sense that if you miss a deadline, you could be responsible for the death of someone. That there's no room for human error. So I think [if I did] something like that, [it] would be just devastating. But sort of setting that aside, I think for me failure would be not trying, not giving it my best."

Gina here is able to define success in terms of her own effort and in terms of living up to her own standards. Others speak of doing something meaningful for their clients. It seems to me that the two thoughts are actually entwined, as Paul's comments show with particular clarity when he explains his feelings after a particular client's execution.

> I'd learned by then that as a defense lawyer what I could do for people that couldn't be taken away was to give them all of me. To not do shortcuts but just, you know, try to do everything in the best way it could be done, because that was a gift to people, and it was something that the client hadn't had before from anybody else. And that at some level, *that* was a contribution I could make to people's lives that meant something to them, that couldn't be taken away, and that was not contingent on whatever the result was.

Paul frames this realization in terms of what cannot be taken away from clients who are about to have their lives taken from them. It's unquestionably a powerful insight in that context. Yet I find that his words further resonate as a summary of what can't be taken away from *him*, or from any of these capital defense attorneys. They have their successes: the triumphs they are able to achieve and the meaning they are able to make along the way. These, too, they carry—if not precisely as compensation for their losses, then certainly alongside them.

CHAPTER 8

# The Relationship

"I MAKE AN effort to focus on what seems to me to be the most important part of the work," Tim says, "which is our relationships with our clients."

Like so many of his colleagues, Tim knows that he will often lose. That's the nature of it. What he has tried to figure out is how to give clients "what they can have in the time they have before they're executed—which is a model of a functional relationship."

This, Tim says, is what he strives to offer. As he talks about trying to give clients an experience of unconditional respect and commitment that is probably unprecedented in their lives, it strikes me that someone overhearing this part of our conversation might guess that I am speaking with a psychotherapist or social worker rather than with a lawyer. I say as much to Tim, remarking that it's interesting to hear a defense attorney frame the value of his work in terms of the healthy relationship he can offer his clients.

"Well, it's one of the only things you *can* give them," he responds. "This is something I can do, and it gives me a way to survive in the work, because it's not about winning or losing anymore."

It's a dual motivation. Focusing on their relationship gives Tim a way to feel that he is doing something helpful and meaningful for his clients, and at the same time it gives him a way to survive in the work, independent of the outcome of the case. In one sense, it's easy to see the liberation that this offers. Looking at it this way, an attorney can derive meaning and feel effective entirely outside of the win-lose axis of the court case.

But in this as in every area of capital defense, the high stakes intensify the experience and, some might also say, the risk. Whatever else it may become, the relationship between capital defense attorney and client is a relationship between one person condemned to death and another who is charged with trying to intervene. Viewing the relationship as the most important part of the work may bring its own set of challenges and questions. For example, are attorneys who define their work this way leaving themselves even more vulnerable to loss and grief?

And perhaps even more immediate, what is it like to forge relationships with people who have committed crimes that, as Simon puts it in Chapter 5, are almost "incomprehensible in their horror"?

It's certainly the core of their practice: representing clients who are guilty of killing other human beings. These are not attorneys who focus primarily on trying to exonerate prisoners claiming innocence. Over their long careers, several of them have indeed represented clients who were found to be innocent as well as clients about whose guilt the attorneys had real doubts. But the drive to uncover and prove wrongful conviction is not all that motivates them or keeps them in the work. When they strive to prevent executions, they know they are more often than not fighting for the life of someone who did commit a terrible crime, someone whom a lot of other people consider monstrous and unworthy of help or care.

"How can you represent people like that?"

It's a question capital defenders get a lot, even from people close to them. Sebastian doesn't mince words when he describes for me his customary response.

"People say all the time, How could you represent a guilty person?" he recounts. "I say, How the fuck could I not? Go back to the eighth grade and read civics."

Sebastian goes on to talk about the clarity of the law: people accused of a crime deserve quality representation. "I've always felt strongly," he says, "that to be someone's representative, what an honor that is. An honor and an obligation."

This principled justification, though also very viscerally felt, gets at some but not all of what it is like to represent people who are guilty of serious crimes. Whatever an attorney might believe at the outset, actually meeting clients for the first time is powerful and often surprising—even, as Gina puts it, "life-changing."

"I didn't have the lay[person's] impression that people in prison are monsters," says Caroline as she recalls her first encounters with prisoners on death row. "But I think we still have a notion, a stereotypical notion of people that we're not even aware of. So when every single time that gets [challenged]—when you're confronted with that unconsciously and see that it's wrong, there's an element of surprise in it."

There are many possible preconceptions that new attorneys, like anyone else, can initially have about death row inmates. One is that those who have been sentenced to the harshest punishment will be the most obviously terrible criminals. Tim remembers his surprise, as a law student, when he discovered that prisoners with death sentences "weren't the worst of the worst. They weren't the most obviously guilty and the most deserving of the harshest punishment. It wasn't clear to me that they had the most culpable intent nor that the killing [they had done] was the worst."

It's always tricky to speak of gradations of horror when, at a basic level, any taking of a life is a devastating act. But some criminals are punished more severely than others, and the small number who get death sentences aren't necessarily the worst. Attorneys can become frustrated and cynical when they realize how random the system is. At the same time, discovering that death row inmates are not necessarily "the worst of the worst" can mitigate the fear that it will be impossible to relate in an ordinary way to someone convicted of a capital crime. Their clients may be at the far end of the spectrum in terms of the punishment they have been given, but the attorneys soon find that this does not necessarily make them the hardest clients to relate to or connect with.

"I remember being struck by how easy it was to chat, how easy it was to find common ground," Roger says of the first death row inmate he met, when he was still a law student. Now, as an experienced attorney, Roger often sends interns to death row simply to meet and talk with clients, because "it's just so eye-opening for law students to see that death row inmates aren't these monsters that are depicted on TV."

Nick remembers being in just that situation. When his boss sent him to death row to meet with a client for the first time, he was struck by how easy it was to relate to the man.

"I remember sitting there talking to him, and it was like, there could be two parallel paths, and in high school he made one choice that went this way, and I made one choice that went that way, and otherwise we were very similar," Nick says. "It sounds like a cliché, but I was just like, 'Oh my God. There but for the grace of God go I.' I remember thinking that."

Simon has a similar memory. "The first time I really came to grips with the fact that I was representing human beings, that this wasn't just a game or an exercise in brief writing or arguing," he says, "was when I first encountered clients that I could really relate to, where I could think, Shit—that isn't anybody that different from me."

As Simon alludes to here, there is a level of post-conviction capital defense work at which it's possible to remain relatively unattached to the people you're fighting for. An attorney can help with legal research or brief writing and be, as Simon puts it, "issue based" rather than "client based." Increasingly, however, good capital defense has come to include extensive research into clients' lives and histories in an attempt to put the pieces together and understand, as Caroline summarizes it, "how they got to where they are." If this sort of investigation is not done at the trial stage, the post-conviction attorneys are motivated to undertake it when they receive the case, not only as an attempt to elicit greater sympathy or understanding for their client, but specifically to demonstrate that, had the relevant information been introduced earlier, a death sentence would have been inappropriate or even unconstitutional. Undertaking this research means that attorneys meet clients' family members, interview people who knew them as children, study school and medical records, and sometimes visit the places where they grew up or otherwise spent time.

"Because of the nature of the work, you don't just know the client, you know the client's life," Caroline explains. It's hard to maintain a one-dimensional view of clients after learning this much about them, the attorneys repeatedly tell me, and it's hard to avoid at least some feeling of intimacy after being allowed to probe so deeply into some of the most painful parts of the client's background. "Trying to understand who they were as human beings," Paul says, "in itself became the thing that was the most compelling [to me]. And it continues to be."

This kind of investigation is compelling not only because of its relevance to the life-saving court battle the attorneys are fighting but also because it becomes a study of some of the most basic and profound of human questions: What makes people who they are? What leads some people to commit terrible acts?

"I started meeting clients and seeing some of the tragedy that is just the name of the game; it's in every case," Simon remembers. "Once I really started living some of this, it was like, my God, what have I gotten myself into?"

Capital defense, it turns out, is not just a legal and procedural thicket. It's also a tangle of human misery, and immersing oneself in it means immersing oneself in stories of poverty, illness, neglect, and abuse. While this may at times make new attorneys want to turn away—"What have I gotten myself into?"—it can also go the other way, so they cannot help being drawn in and affected by what they learn. Simon remembers that one time early in his career he helped with the investigation into the life of a client who had an intellectual disability and had been, as Simon now describes it, "not just badly abused but really tortured by his father." After hearing story after story like this about clients, Simon goes on to say, "You can't, if you have just basic humanity, you can't *not* start to be really affected by the human being you're dealing with."

Being affected on this human-to-human level, however, doesn't necessarily make interacting with clients easy.

"It's impossible not to like some of my clients more than others," says Benjamin. "I think that's kind of shameful because as a lawyer, as an advocate, in your role as the client's champion, you're not supposed to worry about, *the client's an asshole*. It's still your job to save him. And I'm not going to slack; I don't work any less hard because I don't like a particular client. But to pretend that I like all my clients equally would just be nuts."

I don't say this aloud to Benjamin, but it strikes me as more understandable than shameful that a lawyer, like anyone in any helping profession, would privately like some clients more than others. The key, it seems to me, is in what Benjamin says next: that the quality of his work and effort remains constant, even if his responses on a personal level vary. Recognizing clients' humanity arguably means exactly that: not casting them out as evil, but not romanticizing them either.

"Some of my clients are really hard to like," Benjamin continues, "and I'm not even saying that's their fault. Some of them are hard to like because they carry with them the burdens of their unhappy life experiences, which are *so* much more turbulent and traumatic and suffering-filled than mine that I feel guilty about thinking that they're assholes. It's not his fault! I know—but that doesn't make me like him any more."

Some clients are harder to work with than others, and some attachments will be deeper or more personal than others. As Sebastian says,

> You have to do what you need to do in the representation, treat every client ethically and respectfully and professionally, but that being said, not every client is equal in terms of what they mean to you. I like to think, if you're an asshole, I'm still going to do the very best I can. I have a professional obligation to be the best advocate I can be, but I have no obligation to like you. Some of my clients I don't like; most of my clients I like a lot.

These attorneys can hold themselves to a consistent professional standard but can't control the degree to which a client affects them emotionally or how much a client means to them personally. This is a distinction that I think many doctors or teachers might also make. When I listen to the attorneys describe their relationships with clients, I am interested in both kinds of connections: the distinct, personal attachment that sometimes arises between them, as it can between any two individuals, and the circumstantial bond that it seems to me also exists—less personally specific, perhaps, but no less genuine—as a result of the role that the attorney has in the client's life.

Elliot makes this point with particular clarity when he contrasts two clients who were executed in recent years. One, he says, felt like a real friend, someone he "would have had over to my house." The other was someone he didn't like and found it an effort to be with.

"But the point is," Elliot says, "liking [the one client] and not liking [the other] didn't make it any different. The misery was equal [when they were executed]."

"How would you describe the nexus, then?" I ask.

Elliot is silent for several moments.

"I guess it's that one of mine died," he says finally. "Somebody died on my watch."

The impact of the event's being on his watch is so central, Elliot says, that although he feels bad when any execution takes place, when it happens to one of his own clients, "It's almost like, He was mine, and I lost him. It's not a specific sense of failure; it's just the grief of the tribe, the family, or something. They're part of my circle, part of my people, and one of my people died—somebody who's deeply connected to me."

"And that comes from having represented him?" I ask.

"Yes."

The investigation that capital defense teams undertake in order to learn about their clients' lives and backgrounds gives them the awareness that their clients' stories began well before they committed the crime that put them on death row. Representing clients over the course of several years then means that attorneys have the chance to see their clients' stories continue to unfold. "The metamorphosis over the years was incredible," Sebastian says of a client he represented for over a decade, and it was powerful for him to witness that transformation.

Yet for Sebastian and for the others who speak explicitly about this, any pleasure they take in a client's growth over the years is inevitably laced with anger at what they see as the irony of the individual's eventual execution.

"We sentenced him to death," Benjamin says as he summarizes the story of a particular client. "Then we took twenty years to make him into someone whose life was worth saving, and then we killed him. That's the system."

It may be how the system works, but I can hear in their tone that the attorneys don't accept it easily. Keith talks with great feeling about clients who, though "guilty as all get out" of the crimes for which they were sentenced to death, had become, "by the time they were executed, insightful and sensitive people who were contributing, giving people in the community in which they lived. Just the insanity of having those lives taken—it just sort of hits you in a way that you weren't prepared for, however long you were litigating."

It's a paradox that the attorneys find maddening, perhaps all the more so because, through their determined efforts to offer their clients consistent respect and commitment, they may actually help to engender some of the transformation that they're describing. While Tim reminds me of a counselor or teacher when he talks about offering clients a model of a functional relationship, he and several of the others sound even more therapeutically and pedagogically minded when they analyze their clients' behaviors in terms of their previous histories and expectations—specifically, the expectation that no one will stick around for long.

"Almost routinely there's a test," Adam says as he describes this pattern to me. "A moment when they get mad at us and scream and yell at us and tell us to go to hell and get fucked and all this other stuff. It's to see whether we're going to come back or whether we're going to be like everybody else."

It's striking to me that Adam can manage this kind of understanding of what must certainly be a tough experience. But it occurs so reliably with each client, he says, that he has "come to expect it. It always happens."

"So then what?" I ask. "What happens afterward?"

Adam laughs.

A couple of weeks later I'll show back up at the prison, and they'll be astonished and say, "What are you doing here?" I'll say, "I'm your lawyer." They'll say, "Yeah, but I told you to go to hell." You say, "Yeah, I understand, but I'm your lawyer, and people can have disagreements, but that doesn't mean it's the end of the relationship. So, I'm your lawyer, and I'm here, and I'm not going anywhere." And they go, "Wow." After that moment, that's when they start to get a sense of what a real human relationship is.

I can hear in Adam's voice that he delights in foiling clients' expectations in this way. There's something deeply satisfying about it because he recognizes how hungry his clients are for this kind of consistency and because he has managed to decode their message: all that yelling of "go to hell" and "get fucked" is, Adam suggests here, really a way of saying, "Are you going to leave like everybody else?"

Tim describes a pattern that sounds almost identical.

Most of our clients are going to lash out at us at some point or another. And just like when our kids do that, you don't turn around and say, "Oh fuck you, I hate you," right? You say, "OK, are you done with that now? Let's move on." You realize our clients were dysfunctional enough to, in most cases, kill people, sometimes in terrible ways. If we think that some of that dysfunction is not going to manifest in our relationship with the client, we're crazy.

You have to recognize that tendency and not get sucked into it, Tim goes on to say. He acknowledges that maintaining his equilibrium can be especially challenging if a client is astute enough to figure out exactly what will provoke him. "When we get sucked in, it's because of something that's going on with us; someone's hit a button," he says with self-awareness clearly born of experience. "Now, a client could be clever enough to know my weaknesses, to find my buttons, but then you could see that as a strength in the client—you know, Look at that! He's figured something out! Pretty good."

With this perspective, Tim generally manages to maintain his balance with respect to his clients and to hold on no matter how rocky the ride gets.

"I tell my clients, 'I'll be with you 'til you're gone,'" he explains. "I say, 'You can tell me to fuck off; I'll still be with you.' I say, 'You might want to try it now, give it to me now, get it out of the way because I'm not going anywhere.'" In Tim's experience, clients often find that declaration disarming, as it upends their previous expectations in just the way that Adam similarly describes.

Yet none of this means that the relational road is always smooth. "You fill a bunch of roles [for clients], willingly or no," Benjamin observes. As a result, "Clients often burden you with emotional needs that they wouldn't burden you with if they had anybody else, but you're the only one who comes who seems to be affected by their emotional state. So if they're angry, you're the person they're going to pick the fight with. They know that you care, that you'll react."

"Are you in fact affected?" I ask.

"Yes. Of course," Benjamin says, looking at me in surprise. "Well, maybe it doesn't go without saying," he says after another moment. He adds that it can certainly be hard when clients continually try to provoke a reaction.

Standing between clients and the threat of execution, defense attorneys also seem to be right in the line of a lot of emotional fire. They take, and take on, a lot more than the case itself.

"Some days it feels with a client like if I don't keep him alive, he's going to commit suicide," Elliot says, and I am initially taken aback, imagining the burden of feeling that level of responsibility. Attorneys worry that their clients will actively try to take their own lives or will "drop their appeals," which is generally viewed as the passive equivalent. Dropping one's appeals—that is, making the decision not to pursue any further litigation—is the death row inmate's way of saying, *Don't try to stop the train; just let it come.* The possibility that a client will declare that intent is another kind of threat that clearly evokes a lot of feeling in defense attorneys.

It puts them in the position of fighting *everyone* for the client's life—even the client himself.

"I've never represented anybody who didn't talk about dropping their appeals at least once," says Benjamin. "[The clients are saying,] 'This place is so unbearable, and I would rather die than be where I am.' Some are working their way to saying, 'And I'm going to do something about it.' Others are just expressing despair and hopelessness and unhappiness, and I get that. It probably is worse than dying, in some ways, to live on death row."

This is the dubious benefit of "slowing the train down," as I began to explore in the previous chapter. It can make an attorney and client seem at odds about the goal, and I suspect that capital defenders, so focused on saving a life, generally feel they can't countenance the surrender that dropping appeals represents. But the more they speak about these kinds of situations, the more textured I understand them to be.

Keith tells me about a client who "had a death sentence and avoided it by dying of cancer." For Keith, as he thinks about it now, "there's a real sense of victory in that," and I can see how a client's dying on his own terms and in that sense preventing the execution feels qualitatively different not only to the client but also to the attorney. It would thus be too simplistic to say that the attorneys value life over death regardless of the circumstances.

Yet clients' dropping their appeals—choosing to give up the fight against execution—clearly feels harder. As Pamela puts it, "I've said to guys, 'If you want to commit suicide, that's your right, but you can't make us do it. You can't make us involved.' "

The emotional complexity here is that a client's declaration of intent to drop his appeals may be no more pure, no more a final word, than was his "go to hell" test of the attorney's commitment. Dropping appeals may likewise be a test, conscious or not, of whether anyone will care enough to respond. Pamela offers an interpretation that strikes me as analogous to Tim's and Adam's: "I think I make the assumption that all the guys, when they're dropping their appeals, it's [because they feel like], 'Why not? There's nothing here for me.' So my response is kind of a 'yes there is.' Even if it's only me, that's something."

And sometimes Pamela's "yes there is" has tremendous impact. One time, in a particularly acute period of depression and anger, a client told her he was dropping his appeals.

"We got into a screaming match," Pamela recalls. "God knows where the guards were!"

The furor may not have attracted the notice of the correctional officers, but Pamela's outrage did apparently reach the client.

"It was a turning point in our relationship," she says now. "He picked up his appeals. It was like he needed a friend to say, I care enough to stand here and scream at you."

I hear a similar dynamic in Laurel's story about a client who said to her, "I can't live in here. I can't do a life sentence." "What do you do with that?" Laurel wonders aloud as she recounts this for me. At this stage of the process, an attorney fighting to prevent a client's execution is, essentially, fighting to get the client a life sentence instead. Should Laurel have taken her client at his word and not kept litigating? It's a horrendously difficult question, but Laurel says that, ultimately, she "saw what it meant to him to have someone fight for him all the way to the end." Here, again, the client's hope and willingness to stay in the game was not fixed but fluid, and was very much affected by whether someone else seemed to consider him worth fighting for.

It's understandable that seeing someone fight so tenaciously on their behalf and refusing to quit might have a profound effect on death row inmates. But what I also hear in these attorneys' stories is how much it matters to *them* not to give up on a client whom, in their estimation, everyone else has forsaken. It's another aspect of the work that becomes, or perhaps expresses, a deeply held sense of who these capital defenders want to be.

And sometimes, particularly at the very end when—hard as it may be to acknowledge—there is no longer anything to fight, the attorneys can still invoke this "I'm not leaving" principle and recognize that showing up, just being present, is perhaps the one remaining thing they can do. I hear this in Lou's comment that his goal on last phone calls with clients is "making them feel they're not alone." I hear it in Isabel's account of visiting a client (with another lawyer) and being struck by the fact that the client "didn't want to talk about his case. What he really cared about was that we were there and that we cared enough to be there." As she reflects on this, Isabel goes on to say, "A lot of these clients had been there for so long, they knew the system better than we did. They didn't have any illusions that we were going to save them, but it made a difference to them that we were there."

Believing that it is worth something simply to "keep company with the person who hurts," as the writer and psychotherapist Lauren Slater puts it in her book *Welcome to My Country* (New York: Anchor, 1997, 133), an attorney might choose to show up for a client even when that act is not in any other obvious sense productive. Indeed, it seems to me that this belief is the guiding principle influencing attorneys who do choose to witness executions.

When I ask Isabel why she chose to witness a client's execution, she says, "I couldn't not do it." Years before, she had promised the client that if it came to that, she would be there. When the execution was imminent, the client said to Isabel, "I know you promised me, but you don't have to; I release you from that promise." Isabel thought about it and concluded, "I could never live with myself if I didn't. Knowing that you were alone—however bad it's going to be to go through this, it's not going to be nearly as bad as it would be to spend the rest of my life knowing I didn't go."

Although the client had released her from the promise, Isabel felt she would not be able to live with herself if she stayed away. Her commitment to her client, but also to herself, swayed the decision. Laurel, likewise, says, "I had felt for a long time that if my client is going to go through it, the least I can do is be there. . . . I'd always made that commitment to myself."

Those who see the "witness or not" question in this way seem to come to their decision without much struggle or internal debate. At least in those particular instances, they seem to view it as a continuation of the commitment that they made to the client at the start.

"By the time he died, I was his best friend," Elliot says of a client whose execution he witnessed. "It was clear to me, or it felt to me, that he should have somebody on his side there. I did not consider not going to [witness the execution]. It felt like an obligation. Was I scared or ambivalent? Certainly. But not in the sense of, I'm not going to go."

"He needed a friendly face there," Roger explains to me.

"Did he actually express that to you?" I ask.

"I don't think he actually said it, but you could tell. You could feel it."

Roger could feel his client's desire not to go through the execution without the presence of someone who cared about him, even if that desire wasn't explicitly stated. Simon recounts a similar experience when describing a client with severe intellectual disabilities: "My client wanted me to witness—" and then he interrupts himself to clarify, "Well, I say 'he wanted'—he was mentally retarded. He was very damaged, but we talked about it. He had the mindset of a seven- or eight-year-old kid. So I think I led into it by saying, 'I hope it's not going to come to this, but it may, and if it does, I just want you to know that if you want me to be there, I'll be there for you.' I think he very quickly said yes."

Acutely aware of his client's cognitive limitations, Simon felt that he had to be the one to initiate the conversation, and he also felt a particular need to be present given these circumstances. "I was thinking about [my client] as this eight-year-old child and wondering how that would be for a kid to not have anybody there," he says. Simon frames his decision in terms of an assumption of responsibility, and Tim echoes this when he says of a client, "I felt a responsibility to him—that he would not be there by himself [when he was executed]."

Sometimes, of course, a client does explicitly ask the attorney to witness the execution.

"I said, absolutely," Sebastian recalls of the time that this happened to him. "I didn't flinch. I'll be with you. I've been with you the whole time; I'm not going to go away. I was counseled by many good friends not to do it, but actually I think I would have felt worse had I not gone."

Choosing to witness an execution, and, perhaps no less painfully, choosing to delve into the depths of clients' lives to learn "how they got to where they are," means that capital defenders are choosing to encounter some of the roughest and most tragic of human realities. Greater experience with this over time does not necessarily mean the attorneys develop thicker skins, however. As my interviewees chronicle their experiences in capital defense work over many years, they do not always trace an arc from initial vulnerability to greater tolerance for painful stories or horrific details. As we saw in Chapter 5, sometimes the cumulative effect of the work makes aspects of it harder rather than easier to manage over time. In addition, changes in attorneys' own lives, and particularly the experience of becoming a parent, often affect how they absorb this difficult material.

"My tolerance for violence is hugely reduced, especially tolerance for violence to children," Karen says when she compares the experience of doing capital defense work before and after becoming a mother. "Hearing about what [my clients'] childhoods were like—my sense of compassion and horror about that is heightened tenfold. Your sensitivities to things shift," she elaborates. "Before becoming a parent, you can hear about those things and be horrified, but it's not the same as thinking about it in terms of the love you feel for your child, and having a sense of the damage that can be done to a child."

"Does that make you want to recoil?" I ask.

"No," she responds. "I mean, I don't *relish* it, but I have a fuller sense of how important it is. It's painful, it's horrifying, and just so unbelievably sad—"

She trails off, and I think about the fact that even with heightened sensitivity to these horrifying stories of her clients' lives, Karen does not say that she wants to turn away. If anything, she has a greater sense of the need to understand and address the kind of damage she witnesses. At the same time, as she also acknowledges, "sometimes there's a feeling of, Enough already. Enough pain in the world, in my life."

Both can be present: a greater recognition of the importance of what they learn about their clients and, at the same time, a more acute internal response to it. "Imagining something terrible happening to my child—it's the worst thing you can imagine," says Gabe. "If you spend all day long reading cases about people being raped and tortured and that stuff, and you do the thought experiment of putting your own child in the role of the victim, that's—I have to not walk around thinking that it could happen tomorrow to my child."

So it may be, as Gabe suggests, that attorneys have to compartmentalize in order to do the work they do. They may have to develop internal mechanisms in order to keep the full impact of these horrors at bay. Yet what I keep hearing is that there are conflicting pulls: toward self-protection but also toward confrontation with the realities of their clients' stories.

Gabe's comments also introduce another duality of defense attorneys' experience. When Gabe talks about spending all day reading about people being victimized, his words apply both to what has happened to his clients in the past and to what his clients have done. Both stories are often devastating.

"How can you represent people like that?" Even if one accepts Sebastian's point about civics—the basic principles of law and the right of anyone accused of a crime to be ably represented—and perhaps even if one also accepts that prisoners facing death are human beings and not monsters, there is still, inescapably, the fact of what they have done. Usually grisly, terrible, hard to read and even harder to imagine, these facts are part of what attorneys must reckon with.

"I remember reading the [trial] transcript and literally getting up to go to the bathroom to throw up," says Gina of the first capital case she worked on. "It was a terrible crime." Soon afterward, Gina had her first meeting with the client and was struck by both his ordinariness and his humanity. She was forced to hold both realities in her mind: her horror and revulsion at the details of the crime and her horror and revulsion at what the client himself was facing. "I remember sitting at the prison, still sort of naïve, thinking, It's so violent; I can't believe the government wants to kill him. It seemed barbaric to me," she says.

Defense attorneys sit squarely at the intersection of these two realities. "It was a horrible crime. But I loved the client," says Pamela straightforwardly as she recounts a particular story. Pamela here expresses a paradox that is probably as familiar to capital defenders as it is inexplicable to those who may feel that one statement inevitably cancels out the other. What Pamela goes on to talk about, however, is the pull she feels in both directions. This was a case, she remembers, in which she "really identified with the victims." Just as attorneys talk about feeling themselves pulled into the human side of capital defense when they meet clients with whom they can personally identify, so was Pamela powerfully affected by the experience of hearing about victims in such detail, and feeling a connection with them. "You get into the hell that it is to be the victim's family," she says. "I think that's when I really started the recognition that—you've got to remember that there's this side too. I think that really informs my work, and more so every year."

The attorneys who speak in this way about victims and victims' families often refer to a recognition or an increased consciousness that came to them at some point in their careers, rather than an awareness that they had at the outset. Initially their training, and for that matter the basic structure of the legal system, inclined them toward the assumption that allegiances were zero-sum: one could be on the side of either the perpetrator or the victim, but not both.

"I think I understand the experience of victims' families better than I used to," Paul says. "I never *tried* to understand it before." He admits that in the early days of his career, he "just sort of counted [victims' families] as part of the prosecution, and they were all trying to kill my client, and it was a war."

Learning that not all victims' families are in favor of the death penalty may be part of what helped shift this for Paul. But primarily, and much as Pamela describes, the shift occurred as he worked on a case in which the victims' pain was particularly manifest and accessible to him.

"The mindset changed very fundamentally for me," he says. He began wanting to learn about the victims' experiences and even thinking about trying to help victims, though he "felt totally ill equipped and inept and ignorant." He began to make an intentional point of seeking out victims' families, whether in his own clients' cases or in general.

"So at least I've listened to and talked with a lot of survivors and tried to understand," he says now.

Capital defenders' primary obligation is to their clients, and even if they want to take victims' pain into account, it can be challenging to think of how to recognize both perspectives.

"My emphasis over the course of my life has been so much on the pain of my clients and what the government wants to do to them," Adam acknowledges. "I haven't, I don't think, been as sensitive in expressing to you the pain and grief of the victims of violent crime." There are colleagues in the field, he says, who "are really better at that than I am, at getting out really early and up front that they recognize and sympathize with the pain that people who are family members of homicide victims feel. I wish I were somewhat better at that than I am."

Pamela says that after her initial identification with the victim's family in that one particular case, she began to wonder, "How do we approach our work without hurting our client's cause but with a recognition that there's this terrible tragedy, this story over here?"

Sometimes what's at issue is no more and no less than the attorneys' own internal reckoning, their effort to hold both stories in their minds simultaneously. Pamela says that she now makes a point of learning as much as she can about her clients' crimes, not only in order to mount the best defense but also as a way of forcing herself to confront the magnitude of what the client has done. When she looks at autopsy photos and reports of the crime scene, it's because she feels "you have to see this. It's like an obligation: you have to live with it, if you're going to tell [the client's] story. There's this horror on both sides, and so it's necessary for me to—it's only fair that you [the attorney] get this horror before you stand up there all sanctimonious and say, 'Let me tell you what really happened.'"

I suspect that Pamela's determined effort to take in the victims' experience—like Paul's efforts to listen to victims' stories—does permeate her capital defense work and perhaps even affects how she goes about it. Yet maintaining a dual awareness of perpetrator and victim is not easy. As Julian reflects,

> Part of what makes the work so difficult is the dual awareness of the predicament of the client and the damage done by the crime, the horrific things that have happened to the victims in these cases. It's another thing I carry around with me. I have a great desire to see healing for the families that are left behind and justice done for those cases. Maybe my role as a defense attorney at times seems counter to justice being done in cases—but I don't feel that the death penalty is justice. Or maybe it is, but it's also an injustice. I'm certainly conscious, very conscious, of how the successes I may have in at least prolonging my clients' lives may be having the effect of [upsetting] a whole 'nother set of people. My heart goes out to them, and the images of their dead children and parents and siblings float in my head, and I feel the same degree of anger and outrage.

It's a duality keenly felt and with no clear resolution. Sometimes the awareness itself—the attempt to recognize and feel the impact of both tragedies—is the most that an attorney can do.

"He was screaming, *I'm human! I'm human!* as he was being executed," Laurel says. She is describing one of the first executions that took place after she began doing capital defense work. A flood of images accompanies the story: Laurel and the other attorneys at the prison in the deepest middle of the night; her colleagues' faces as they exit the prison after witnessing the execution; the drive home afterward, and Laurel's feeling of disconnection from the ordinary world. Yet after hearing Laurel's story, it's this scream from the condemned prisoner that stays with me and keeps repeating itself in my mind. And I'm not the only one. "It *really* affected me," Laurel says quietly.

It seems doubly emblematic, somehow: a client's desperate assertion of his humanity and the attorneys' encounters with it, not just in that final moment but so often and in so many ways. When they speak of their clients' humanity, there is often a sense that the attorneys feel themselves to have seen something, experienced something, that they are unsure of being able to convey fully. It can't be easy to know what they know about their clients. It can't be easy to feel that they have to defend not only their clients' lives but also their dignity. Yet it's clear that the attorneys are deeply affected and even changed by seeing the humanity of people who have committed terrible crimes.

"In a way I think it's made me a more compassionate person," Gina says. "I don't see things so black and white. I think having compassion for someone who commits a terrible act is something that doesn't come easy, and I think it makes you a better person if you can get there and maybe not have such a sense of hatred inside."

Talking about a client—eventually executed—to whom he had gotten especially attached, Sebastian says, "I think I'm a better person for having known [the client]."

I ask how he means that.

"I hope more caring, more insightful—that kind of thing," he says. "And more willing to put myself out and to be hurt."

I am struck by his assessment, which seems to have a resonance far beyond his work as a lawyer. I say as much, and Sebastian agrees, adding, "But I think part of being a good lawyer is you've got to be a good human. I think they're intertwined."

So they are. And so it often happens that working this way, forging these kinds of relationships with their clients, the attorneys become deeply and personally attached to the people they are representing.

"I can bring myself to tears just driving down the road and thinking—oh, you know, it's like when any good friend dies," Pamela says as she tries to answer my question about what brings back memories of clients who have been executed. "When you're on your own, that's when it always hits you. These guys are gone, but they were so much a part of my life."

For all the times that clients can be manipulative or difficult, for all the testing and lashing out, for all the unique demands that this high-stakes relationship creates, there is also a sense in the attorneys' stories of what is uniquely rewarding about attorney-client relationships. *"I learned so much from him." "I considered him a friend." "Every time I get involved with clients, and get insight about their lives, I feel like I have grown."* I hear statement after statement like this. In and among the other aspects of the loss they suffer when a client is executed, some measure of that loss is, simply, personal.

Nick tells me that friendships with clients are the heart of the work for him. I remark that arguably there are many ways to make good friendships, so perhaps there is something distinct about this context or this kind of relationship that appeals to him.

"I don't like making friends," Nick replies with a smile. "It's odd—I don't know—maybe because I don't need—maybe it's because I make all my friends on death row!"

He laughs again at his own statement, then continues, "I don't particularly like to go out among a lot of people, a bunch of people I don't know. I don't make new friends. And I guess maybe it's because I find most people in social settings to be not very genuine. [In this context] you sort of cut through all that. It is what it is here. You know, he's in the worst possible position, and you're there to help him or do what you can. It's very defined roles, I guess."

The relationship between defense attorney and client is both clearly defined and undiluted by usual social niceties. The urgency and clarity yield an authenticity that either reduces or is a result of the attorneys' already lowered tolerance for more superficial interactions.

Sebastian says people in his life describe him as "socially introverted," but he has noticed that clients bring out another side of his personality.

"It's kind of a weird paradox," he says. "I think I'm introverted in a way. I don't like conflict personally. But if I'm representing you, I can spit in somebody's face; I can be confrontational. I don't like it in my own life, but if I'm doing it for you, that's fine; I'm being your advocate."

"You can do for someone else what you might not do for yourself," I observe.

"Right. It's my job. I'm supposed to do it. I'm required to do it. If I can't do it, I shouldn't be in the game."

I'd guess that if I were interviewing other helping professionals I might very well hear similar sentiments—both the preference for substantive conversation over small talk and the readiness to do for others what they may be less likely to do on their own behalf.

At the start of this chapter, I raised the possibility that attorneys who put so much emphasis on their relationships with clients might be making themselves even more vulnerable to loss and grief when their clients are executed. Without question, the losses hit them hard—the loss of any client, as we have seen, but especially those to whom they have formed a close personal attachment.

"I was there with him all day until five minutes before he was executed," says Adam, describing for me his last hours with a client who meant a great deal to him. The two men sat talking together on opposite sides of the cell bars for hours. Adam continues,

"The warden comes down and says it's time for the execution, and they were going to take him through that door—"

Adam motions across the length of the small room where we are having our interview, to show me how close to the execution chamber he and his client had been having their final visit. "We get up, and the warden reads, 'Having been found guilty of first-degree murder, the laws of [the state] and the jury have duly sentenced you to death,' you know, blah blah blah, all this bullshit, and I say to the warden, 'Can I give him a hug?' He says, 'No, we don't want him to get upset emotionally.'"

Adam pauses. "It was a very, very painful no," he says, his voice breaking. "To be told I couldn't give him a hug. I'll never forgive that man for saying no."

He tells it so vividly that I'm inside the moment, feeling some measure of the connection Adam felt with his client, the acuteness of the loss, and the added insult of being denied the chance to mark the end in this natural, human way.

Adam didn't witness this client's execution.

"I desperately wanted to be there for him when he was executed, and he just as desperately insisted that I not be. I had said to him, 'I want you to have someone there whose eyes you can look into and know that that person who's looking at you loves you.' And he said, 'I know. But I care too much for you to have you be there. I don't want you to have to see that.'"

They argued back and forth about it, but ultimately, Adam says, it was the client's decision. So Adam stayed as long as he was allowed to, right up until those moments before the execution. I ask what he believes he is trying to do during a last visit like that.

"Well, I think the prison sees me as their representative at that point—to try to keep him occupied and calm. I guess at that point [it could be argued that] I'm an agent of the state. But really, you know, the bottom line is you're sharing a human experience with a guy you've come to care about over the course of years."

I ask Adam if he ever regrets making his relationships with his clients so central to his work. He responds,

> I feel like it *is* central to my work. I feel like I can't advocate for my clients as well unless I really know them intimately. And maybe even if that were not true, I wouldn't want to do it any other way anyway. It's just sort of the way I approach the world. It may be that there are ways to insulate oneself from the emotional pain if you don't get so close to somebody during the time you're representing them, but that's not the way I *want* to do business, and it's just not the way I do it.

Technically speaking, it might be a choice, but the way Adam and so many of the others express it, becoming attached to their clients is so intrinsic to their way of working, to their sense of themselves as defense attorneys, that the alternative doesn't feel truly viable.

"What about the argument that if you didn't get so close to them, it would be easier?" I ask Pamela after she tells me about being brought to tears by memories of her clients who have been executed.

"Yeah, people say that," she nods. "I say, That's the way I do it. That's just the way I do it. That's how I need to do it, how I want to do it."

It's hard to tell whether this is a personal need or a need derived from Pamela's assessment of what constitutes quality representation. The two often become intertwined for Pamela and the other attorneys.

"I was probably too attached," Nick says of a client who, as he puts it, "became more than a client—he became a friend."

I repeat the phrase back to him: "*Too* attached?"

"Well, not for me. I wouldn't trade those years for anything."

The "too," it appears, is in comparison to a possible external notion of what a lawyer should be like rather than an expression of Nick's own regret or self-recrimination. Later in the interview I ask Nick the same question I've asked the other attorneys: "What would you say to the argument that if you didn't get so attached, it wouldn't be so hard?"

"It *should* be hard," Nick responds with ready emphasis. "If you didn't get attached to them, you might not do everything you needed to do."

The rationale, then, is both personal and normative. Roger, too, feels so strongly about this that he responds to my question with obvious incredulity in his voice.

"You can't do this work and not be attached on a human level to your client," he says. "I mean, you *shouldn't* do it if you're not attached."

"Why not?" I ask.

"Because we are the ones taking care of our clients. We are the ones standing between them and the machinery of death, and if we join in the line vilifying them, how can we possibly get out there and advocate for saving them? You've got to feel this work; you can't just think it."

"In order to do it well, you mean?"

"In order to do it well, and in order to have any kind of credibility with your client."

"Is any part of that about how you yourself want to do it?" I ask.

"It's never struck me as how I *want* to do it," he responds. "I always thought of it as, it's the only way to do it. There is no alternative way to do it. I mean, if you can't see the humanity in your client, how can you advocate, how can you convince somebody else to see the humanity?"

"Is there a difference between seeing their humanity and getting personally attached?" I wonder aloud.

"Ultimately, they're going to need to feel a personal connection with you to share the details of their lives," Roger says, now focusing on what some might see as the practical or even strategic benefits of forging a trusting relationship with a client.

"Are there costs to you in that?" I ask, bringing the question back to his own experience one final time. Roger is silent a moment and then responds, "I guess at the end. But I mean—it seems like having human connections isn't necessarily a *cost*."

I'd pursued the point not because I actually doubted what Roger was saying but because I wanted to get as close as possible to the heart of his beliefs about the risks of becoming so attached to clients who will very likely be executed. His answer is both succinct and profound, and it summarizes what so many of his colleagues also feel. Yes, the risk is great. The loss is, and cannot help but be, tremendous. But in capital defense as in any endeavor, the human connections are both the gift and the point.

# CHAPTER 9

# Getting Out

For every person you've met who's done this work for a long time, there are probably five or ten more who only did it for a couple of years and then moved on. –Gabe

I've seen people in this work kill themselves through the stress. I can name half a dozen people whom we've lost. –Lou

I can definitely see other people really suffering. . . . There's a lot of that in the death penalty lawyer community. Do you blame it directly on the work or not? It's a lot easier to for me to see it in others than it is to see it in myself. –Simon

We saw in Chapter 6 that there are all sorts of reasons capital defenders might want to avoid scrutinizing how their work affects them. Here's another possibility: there may be a worry that if they examine the matter too carefully, they might have to reconsider doing the work at all, or they might have to justify it to the people in their lives who ask, "Why do you do it if it affects you that way?"

The question of quitting can be volatile. Long-time capital defenders notice the colleagues who have left. They notice with curiosity ("I wonder what that would be like") or occasional envy ("He did what I've dreamed of doing")—but that's if the leaving seemed deliberately chosen. Stories of colleagues who *had* to get out, who burned out or imploded and couldn't go on, are obviously more frightening. In a real sense they constitute more losses. Getting out, quitting, wanting to quit, having to quit—all this lives in the minds of even those attorneys who have stayed committed to the work for years and years.

"There's a part of me that would like to stop doing this," Paul says about halfway through our interview.

"What does that part say?" I ask. "What would it be like to stop?"

"I could breathe again."

Paul's response took *my* breath away, so vividly did it let me glimpse his current experience. If you want to know what something is like for someone, ask what he imagines it would be like not to do it. All their comments help to create a picture of what capital defense is like for these attorneys, but hearing them muse about what it would be like to quit—no matter how unlikely they are to act on that fantasy—opens a very particular kind of window.

"Does it ever cross your mind to quit?" I ask Pamela after she has been talking about the second-guessing and the feeling of exhaustion—almost like being hung over—that comes after clients' executions.

"And sell lampshades?" she responds, laughing. "Every day! I mean, who doesn't want a job that when you clock out, you're gone?"

*When you clock out, you're gone* is about as different from the internal experience of capital defense as possible, so I can see why the contrast is intriguing.

"I think about it, but not all that seriously," Eric responds when I pose the same question.

"What's the thought about?"

"It's about going and being a file clerk somewhere and—alphabetizing!"

He bursts out laughing; the idea is so preposterous or so different from his current daily life. I ask what he imagines life would be like as a file clerk.

"Going to work, coming home, and it's over," he says immediately.

"Day's over, nothing to do now, go and do whatever I want. No thoughts popping in, nothing troubling you. That's definitely the allure."

These are manifestly not the kinds of jobs they've chosen: jobs that let you clock out at night and not be haunted later on by worry or doubt or grief. But they think about it sometimes; they let themselves imagine an entirely different kind of life.

There's the allure of work that is over at the end of the day, but I also hear in their responses a curiosity about work that might deliver a more easily felt sense of accomplishment and effectiveness.

"I think one of my fears is that what I know is very limited," Benjamin says. It takes me a moment to imagine what he might mean by this, because what I'm initially aware of is how knowledgeable he is and how much others respect him for that knowledge. I wonder if he's exhibiting the kind of self-doubt that is often described as "imposter syndrome"—a highly accomplished person worrying that people will find out that he doesn't know as much as it appears. But as I listen further, it becomes clear that's not quite what Benjamin means.

> My legal skills are so highly specialized. It's like being an alchemist: you know something really well that's highly arcane and may be vanishing at any time because it's totally a social construct. I often say, "I wish I could join pipes or bake bread," because I feel like then I would really know something. Because I feel like what I know is all abstract and abstruse and human-made and could be swept away tomorrow if the courts or Congress decided they wanted to change everything. But if you're a plumber, you can fix a drain today, tomorrow, and forever.

I hear Benjamin expressing a longing for something more concrete and externally verifiable—and, perhaps, for an enterprise that would not require its practitioners to work so hard to find a definition of success they can live with. Benjamin continues,

"That's the thing that I think deep down inside is my gnawing fear:

that people will find out that what I know is really pretty limited and has so little connection to the real world."

"People will find out," I say, repeating his phrase. "But it sounds like *you're* wondering about it too."

He nods. "I do wonder. When I think about doing something other than death penalty work, for the most part I don't think about other kinds of law practice. I think, I'll go and learn how to install solar panels! I like that idea. I like the idea that you do something constructive. It's good for the planet, it helps people, and requires some actual knowledge."

It's interesting to me that he again makes the distinction between his kind of expertise and actual—concrete and physical—knowledge. He goes on to say,

> It's not that I don't love being a lawyer, but when I imagine myself doing something else, it's not another kind of law. I imagine doing something else altogether. Being a housepainter! You paint a house, and the house looks a lot better. It's something you can control, and when you're done, you can say, Look at that house! It's now been preserved for another five to ten years, and it makes the residents happier, and it makes the neighborhood look nicer. And I'm going to wash my hands off, and tonight I don't have to worry about painting this house—tomorrow I'll paint a different house. That's the kind of thing that appeals to me as a model for what I'd like to do.

Why *not* paint houses, then, or do anything else that might let them breathe more easily?

Part of the answer lies in all the reasons these attorneys give for getting into capital defense in the first place, all the ways it satisfies them and feels like vital work. When I ask Pamela how she talks back to those daily thoughts of quitting capital defense to sell lampshades, she says, "The talk back is, But when it feels good, it feels *so* good. When it works, it works so well. The [client] is still sitting there talking on the phone to you because you did it; you [stopped the execution]."

Once again, the high stakes are what make capital defense both so tough and so compelling. But there are other factors, too, that make quitting difficult.

"As a practical matter I can't [quit] because there's nobody else [in this state] who could take my clients," Paul says. Others express their own version of this: it's hard to abandon clients midstream.

"I have thought about not doing [this work] many, many times," Simon admits. "I tried to get out—"

He interrupts himself and laughs, saying, "It sounds like being an addict." As Simon continues to describe various points in his career when he entertained the notion of reducing his caseload or getting out of capital defense entirely, his words echo Paul's. Given the gravity of the responsibility he feels, Simon explains, "It's hard to try to extricate yourself in a way that's responsible to the client."

"I joke about habeas work being like the Mafia," says Roger. "You know that old line, 'You try to get out, and they keep pulling you back in.'"

Roger had some years ago changed law offices so that he would be in a position to take on a variety of criminal cases, not just death penalty cases. He did find it a great relief to have access to that variety, but he also found that he kept more capital cases than he had anticipated.

"I took a couple of [capital] cases with me, because if not me, who? It just didn't make sense to have cases that I'd worked on [at one stage] and then when it came to [a later stage] just not be there for them."

Keith's experience is similar. He, too, switched law offices years ago, imagining that he would then do much less capital defense work. "But I just never got away from it," he says with the same wry laugh I hear from the others who speak about this. "My thought was, I will wind down these cases . . . but it just never worked out that way. I kept too many of the post-conviction cases with these long lives, and then this case came along, and that case came along, and before you know it, all these years later I've done as much capital work as I did before."

It might theoretically be possible to say no to a case at the outset, but getting out of it once you're invested and responsible is much harder.

"What do you do, give them back?" Pamela asks rhetorically. "I've never been any good at that."

At one point, Pamela seriously believed she was going to get out of capital defense.

"I can't do this," she remembers feeling. "I can't watch these guys die." It was after a recent spate of executions, and Pamela remembers "driving down to the prison and thinking, I don't want to go here. I can't do this. They've killed all of you. I can't watch these guys die."

She pauses, and I wonder how the story will end, knowing that as we sit here today, Pamela still has clients under death sentences. She continues:

"But the problem is, I kept their damn cases. I didn't give anybody up! Well, there are some cases I didn't keep, but mostly—"

She trails off, contemplating this.

"So now I'm sitting here," she says as if in conclusion. Sitting here, anticipating the very thing she had said she couldn't face.

"It's interesting," I say, "all that feeling of, 'I can't do this' but then not getting out."

Pamela laughs again in rueful acknowledgment. "It's just a personality flaw." After another moment she adds, "It's also that I don't want to be another one of the people who has refused to stick with them. I don't want to be another person who leaves."

"So you've got the risk of the very thing you said you couldn't do— have more clients executed?"

"Yes. I know." She nods. It is simply true, without resolution.

Though some attorneys have visions of completely different kinds of work, others say they can't picture themselves doing anything else.

"I can't even imagine what else I could do," Gina says when I ask if she ever thinks about quitting. "I honestly can't think of anything else I would want to do. I think I'm doing what I love to do—what will I do when I can't work anymore?"

Similarly, when I ask Nick, he says, "No. There's not been a day in twenty years when I've felt, I don't want to go to work. I get paid to do something I would do for free. It's like playing baseball—that'd be the next best thing."

Sometimes the "no" seems to come from attorneys' being unable to imagine themselves, in particular, doing anything else. Since Karen had spoken so vividly of the pain of clients' executions, I ask if stopping has ever occurred to her. She shakes her head no.

"It's what I do," she says. "I think it's extraordinary work that needs to be done, and I've gained some experience doing it. And—what the hell would I do?" She laughs. "There's a literal sense, because it's all I've ever done as a lawyer, but also—what do you do after this?"

In Karen's phrase "it's what I do" I hear an identification with the work that also comes through in Paul's comments.

"Maybe there is a kind of addiction to doing this, because I don't know what I would do if I didn't do this," he says. "I *think* I would think of things to do. I mean, there are plenty of other things in the world that need to be addressed—"

He pauses for a moment and then continues, "I do think that I'm sort of—I'm conditioned to need to do something for somebody else. I certainly believe in lots of good work that other people do, but I can't imagine me doing that instead of doing this."

Simon jokes about sounding like an addict, and here Paul raises the same question. I think of the attorneys' references to being "adrenaline junkies." They wonder themselves, sometimes, why they were originally drawn to capital defense and why they feel so compelled to stay with it. I suspect that it can be hard to sort questions about the initial draw of capital defense work from questions about its enduring hold on those who stay with it. You can have a temperament that draws you to high-stakes, high-intensity work, as some speculate in Chapter 2. But it's also possible that the "adrenaline high" itself fosters the craving for more.

"I've heard it several times," Simon tells me. "The idea of the fix mentality: You thrive on being in this role. You obviously get something out of this."

"It's interesting," I say in response. "The phrase 'get something out of it' is sort of morally neutral, psychologically neutral, right? But it depends on the tone. People don't tend to do things they don't get anything out of, after all."

"Right," Simon agrees. "Of course. So the question is whether what you're getting out of it—is it good to get that out of it? Is it a trap because you can't stop doing it, like an addiction?"

These are rich questions, and I don't hear Simon answering them definitively for himself as we speak. He knows he has many times thought about getting out but has never taken serious steps toward that possibility. He knows that capital defense still means a great deal to him, even after years of practicing.

"I don't know," he says as he continues to muse about all this. "I still think this work is important, really good stuff, really honorable. There's probably some self-delusion. I'm sure I do 'get something out of it,' benefit myself from it, but, you know—it's hard to separate all that out."

"Is there anything you would miss if you quit?" I ask.

"Yes, absolutely," he responds immediately. "I think I get reward—somewhere deep down inside I feel like—well, I sleep really well at night. Which is sort of a simplified way of saying I feel really good about the choice I've made from an ethical or moral perspective. Like, at least I've stayed true to my moral principles. That does make me feel good."

Some attorneys reflect on how they will know when it is finally time to stop.

"There was a client I was really close to," Gabe says, for example, "and I had resolved that if he was executed, I would stop [doing this work]. It was too much. I got serious migraine headaches in the time leading up to the execution date. I felt the pressure on that one."

Gabe mounted an enormous legal and public relations campaign for this client that, against all odds, was effective; the client is now serving a life sentence instead of death. "Part of what drove me," Gabe explains, "is that the errors [in that case] were so outrageous. I felt, If I can't win this one, either I'm not a good enough lawyer to be doing this, or there's no point in doing it because the system is so corrupt."

Listening to Gabe recount this, I am acutely aware that it could have gone the other way. As we have seen, even with outrageous errors and highly skilled post-conviction capital defense attorneys, clients still do get executed. I hear Gabe expressing his own sense of where he draws the line and what feels to him like too much to bear—whether in terms of pressure or in terms of the futility of his efforts.

I hear something similar in Karen's description of a current case. She doesn't say she will quit if this client is executed; she doesn't even imply it. What echoes Gabe's thoughts, for me, is Karen's sense that losing this particular case would be, in some way, too much.

"If he gets executed, I will feel like a failure," she says. "It will feel like something could've, should've been done. It will be so wrong if he gets executed. I will be horrified. I dread that, how horrible I will feel."

"What do you do with that dread?" I ask.

"I work very hard, I guess."

I tentatively suggest that in addition to working very hard for the obvious reason that she desperately wants to prevent this execution, she might also be hoping to avoid having to feel so horrible.

She shakes her head. "I don't think of it that way, no. I'm just cognizant that I can't lose this one."

I tell her I see the difference and drop the point. We sit in silence for a moment.

"Maybe it is that," she says suddenly. "Maybe it *is* I can't lose this one because I won't be able to live with myself. Maybe there is a piece of that, yes."

Some of the attorneys speculate that they might possess a finite amount of energy for capital defense, or a finite ability to keep doing it well.

"If I get to the point where either other people recognize—or I recognize first—that I'm not doing it very well—" Paul muses, "I mean, if I get to that point, I can stop, because I know that that will not help people."

Whether he or someone else makes it, a convincing assessment that he is no longer effective at helping people would persuade Paul to get out of capital defense. But "I'm not there yet," he says, and he can't predict when that point might come or "if it will be before I die."

Benjamin isn't there yet either, but he has a sense of what it might be like to feel that he has reached the limits of his own resources. He says,

> I think I have a finite number of death penalty cases in me. I don't know what the number is, and I don't know how much warning I'll have before the meter turns over to zero. I really think I might wake up one morning—I mean, if they kill [the client whose case I'm heavily involved with now], I could wake up the next morning and say, I'm done. That's it. I'm going to get other people on my cases, and I'm going to quit and do something else. Just because I think you can only go to so many funerals.

After another moment, Benjamin qualifies his general statement, saying that maybe *he* can only go to so many funerals. He names other capital defenders who strike him as having a greater capacity. "There are people in our community who I feel have a bottomless well of strength and serenity," he says.

As I listen to him I marvel at the way so many of the interviewees seem to think other capital defenders possess greater equanimity than they themselves do. It shows how deeply they respect and admire each other; it is also another indication of how unaccustomed they are to speaking openly about all the times that they feel neither strong nor serene.

"I don't have that," Benjamin continues, distinguishing himself from those who appear to have a bottomless well. "My well is—I can hear the bucket splashing at the bottom every time it goes in, and I just don't know how many more times it's going to come up with anything in it."

Later in our interview he returns to this image.

> I think that I conceive of my own resources that I bring to the work as being my life force, my energy, my skills such as they are. Just in

my mind, the way I conceive of that, it's like a life force. My energy and my desire to do things flow through me and from me into my clients. That's why the well metaphor has always worked for me. It's a sense of, I go to this source of energy and will, and I draw from it in order to keep going. But I have a sense that every time I have to do that, it's not coming up overflowing. The bucket's rattling around, and it's coming up half full of mud now, you know?

I nod. It's a poignant glimpse into his experience.

Though he had a moment ago suggested that he might wake up one morning and find himself done with the work, he goes on to speak, as others have, of the difficulty of giving cases up midstream. "The bucket's not completely empty," he says. "I'm staying in the game."

While they stay in the game, the attorneys do have some practical options for varying the way they play it. They can sometimes choose to cut back on the number of capital cases they take on or make other kinds of adjustments to the way they engage in the work.

Eric initially chose to engage in "crisis litigation"—taking on cases at the end stage, when almost all legal options have already been exhausted. The work was compelling to Eric because he could see that these were the clients in greatest need. Yet as the term suggests, this kind of litigation is particularly demanding and keeps an attorney's adrenaline running high.

"I'm beginning to be more careful about what I get involved in," Eric says now. "Not getting involved in a case now unless there's a good team to work with, because being the only one who knows a case is one of the most difficult things. I want to be very vigilant about that."

Karen, similarly, says she has "tried to shift things to minimize my involvement in last-minute work. The toll was too great on my life," she explains.

Sebastian uses the same phrase—the toll was too great—to explain his decision not to take on another long-term post-conviction capital case at this point in his career. Knowing that these cases can last ten or fifteen years, he says, "I'm not convinced that at my age I want that again."

He doesn't regret doing it before, though.

"I think in my formative years it probably was a good thing, because it helped mold my character and helped mold who I am as a lawyer," he says.

To Sebastian, the stress inherent in long-term representation of clients facing execution seems built in: "If it didn't take a toll on you, then there's a problem; you probably shouldn't be doing it, quite frankly. So, OK, if by definition it has to take a toll, I'm willing to let that happen, but I just don't want to do it all the time. I want to limit the number of [capital] cases I'm involved in."

As described in Chapter 5, Adam was so affected by a series of clients' executions that he hit a wall of paralysis and felt himself unable to work; he ultimately recognized that it was that "end-stage" work that was so particularly emotionally challenging for him. He says, "One of the things I realized was: I need to take a break from post-conviction work, because my body and my head are telling me that I'm freezing, that I can't do this. So if I want to keep doing capital work, I'd better go to another part of capital work where I don't have to be there at the end of the process."

Adam switched for a while to working at the appellate rather than post-conviction stage, meaning he took cases at an earlier point in the process. "Instead of doing the last round, I was doing the very first appeal after trial," he explains.

"Was that indeed what the doctor ordered?" I ask.

"Yes, very much so. I had said to myself, I need to get away from the end of the process, but I want to keep doing this work because this work is important to me."

One could say that Adam didn't, at first, consciously decide to change his approach to capital defense work. His freezing up and being unable to work essentially forced him to pay attention and then respond in some way. Isabel, too, describes in Chapter 5 an experience of paralysis one evening while working at her computer. As a result of that tough night, Isabel continued working only on cases that did not involve an immediately pending execution, and she eventually tapered off even more than that. "I said, I'm just not doing that anymore," she explains. For Isabel, the cost to herself had become too high.

Laurel reached a similar point. "I thought I would never stop doing death penalty work," she says. "I thought that's who I was." But after the loss of several clients, her thoughts became: "I can't do this anymore. I can't invest myself in another person and another case, starting from the beginning and putting myself into it and going through all those stages of loss—because of what this has done to me. There's nothing else there to give. If I'm going to be happy in life, I can't do that work anymore."

Often, the cumulative stress and grief affects the attorneys in ways that their bodies demonstrate before they let themselves acknowledge it in words.

"You can go along doing this stuff for quite some time, if your body allows," Julian says. "My body was beginning to tell me that I was beginning to wear out."

Julian's realization was more gradual than the all-at-once hitting-a-wall moments I've just described, but it was powerful nevertheless.

"I think there is a way people process this work," Julian continues, "and it's not a good way: instead of listening to the body, just pouring yourself into something new, work-wise. So I just worked myself to the bone."

Others speak about paralysis—the sudden inability to work—and Julian is talking about working non-stop, yet each phenomenon is a reaction to the emotional effects of what they experience.

"I thought of it as changing pastures," Julian goes on to say, speaking of his habit of pouring himself into the next case immediately, without respite. "You know, you move from one to the next in order not to become bogged down. I think that had its positive aspects, because my energy didn't turn negative; I would just keep re-channeling it. But I nearly wiped myself out with work."

Julian's body began to tell him that this practice wasn't sustainable. He also began to worry that his work and its effects on him were in turn affecting his family. "Questions were beginning to dawn on me about whether what I was doing was harmful to the family," he recalls now.

With this combination of exhaustion and tentative awareness that things might need to change, Julian began to "step back and say, I don't need to be doing all this; I can start choosing how I approach this system."

If one wants to choose how to approach the work, or the death penalty system, options are sometimes available. A few attorneys talk about working on cases as consultants, rather than as the attorney with the direct responsibility. One, for example, describes gradually cutting down on his caseload and doing mostly consulting after over a decade of intense work as a capital defender. "My body was giving out," he says of that time period, echoing the observations that others make about the work's physical toll. "I probably drank too much. I didn't have healthy ways of coping and wasn't thinking about trying to take care of myself. If you let it, this work can really take over your life."

During that intense period, he missed a lot of family events, which he now regrets. "It's too much to sacrifice," he says. "But on the other hand, [in the midst of it] it's hard to say, I'm not going to write this pleading because [I have an event to go to]."

These are the tensions that, as this attorney suggests, can perhaps be lessened, if not fully resolved, by changing the nature or extent of one's responsibility to a case. The relative anonymity of working as a consultant can reduce the feeling that the client and the client's family are desperately looking to him to prevent the execution. At the same time, even as a consultant, he often feels responsible enough that he'll jump in and even essentially ghostwrite the legal material if he sees the attorney of record making errors or failing to take advantage of key opportunities. The habits of the kind of capital defense he has engaged in for so long are hard to break. Still, he says, consulting does generally feel easier.

Caroline, too, talks about doing more consulting than direct representation these days. Partly as a result of this, it's been a while since she has had to experience a client's execution.

"I think that once I [made that switch], I'm slower to take it back on," Caroline observes. "If you have a choice to stay somewhat distanced from it and not overwhelm yourself with that kind of pain, it's easier."

Arguably, Caroline had that choice all along, from the moment she decided to undertake capital defense instead of any other endeavor. But, Caroline acknowledges, it's harder to feel a sense of choice when in the thick of the pressure and intensity. Stepping out of that maelstrom can make space for a new kind of reflection and deliberation. She goes on to offer this analysis:

> I think early on, when you are so driven for whatever reasons, you're really in the middle of it, and you're invested in a way that doesn't hold anything back, which is one of the things that makes it so hard. You develop really close relationships [with clients], and you're not cautious for yourself. You do suffer a lot of losses, and it is really hard emotionally and physically and all ways; it's really hard to go through that. And then if you reach the point where you have choices, or make choices, and you're not thrown into it day after day . . . there for me has been a reluctance to open myself back up to it—and that's not conscious. I'm reluctant to take a case, but I don't consciously say that that's the reason. I don't create situations where I get to know people. I work on cases where I don't get to know the client. I still am doing work that I really like and that energizes me, but I'm not making myself vulnerable.

These are attorneys for whom getting attached to clients, and in that sense making themselves vulnerable to loss, is the preferred way to practice capital defense. As we saw in Chapter 8, this is how they do it and how they believe in doing it. At the same time, comments like Caroline's reveal that there is an awareness of the cumulative effect of this kind of experience, and attorneys sometimes make a choice—however conscious or not—to shift the balance and act in more self-protective or self-preserving ways. It reminds me of the attorneys who have decided not to witness executions (at all, or anymore): it's the drawing of a line, making a choice about what to take on or take in. Some attorneys who have been practicing for years or even decades explain that their more recent choices in this regard differ from those they made at an earlier time in their lives and careers.

Lou, like Caroline and so many others, gives high priority to relationships with clients, and over his career as a capital defender, he has lost many. He says that these days he sometimes limits the number of clients to whom he becomes emotionally attached, or even the number with whom he has direct contact.

"[There are times now when] I could have taken a phone call from a guy who was going to be executed," says Lou of cases at the very final stage for which he is helping with the legal work. "And I say, No, I don't want that. I don't know him, and I want to keep it that way."

When Lou makes this choice now, it's precisely because he understands from experience how painful an execution is when he has gotten to know the client.

"It's so completely different when you know the person," he says. "As horrible as it is when you *don't* know the person, as ghoulish and ghastly and all the horrible things about it, when you have met the person or know their full humanness, it's just so much more. It has so much more impact, is so much more meaningful to you. So sometimes I don't take the call. I say, No thank you. He's going to be executed in a week. I don't need to feel that additional pain."

Stepping back and choosing how to approach the work can create space for reflection, as Caroline suggests, and can also give rise to an impulse to pass on what they have learned. Some of these experienced capital defenders have turned to legal teaching as they have cut back on their caseloads (or, sometimes, on top of quite full caseloads). One of the attorneys laughs as he tells me that he thought teaching might be easier than practicing law, but in fact it is in its own way as demanding, or at least as time-consuming. Still, he says the experience is valuable to him.

Teaching is good because each semester you get a crop of fresh and interested students and [as you explain the system and hear students' reactions], it keeps you shocked at the things you should be shocked at—so you don't end up jaded and just letting things slide. It helps you maintain that sense of, This is wrong, and it doesn't matter that it's been happening every day for twenty years and is going to happen again tomorrow—that doesn't make it right. The students help keep it fresh.

After years of immersion in the world of the death penalty, it's not only the law or its procedures that capital defenders find themselves wanting to convey to others, however. There is also all the humanity they've come in contact with—so powerful for the attorneys and, in their eyes, so often misunderstood. Some attorneys imagine or have already begun to engage in other, non-legal means of telling the stories they have come to know and understand over the years: writing for different kinds of audiences, giving public talks, and creating documentary films or other video presentations.

"One of the things [all this work] makes me want to do is figure out how to communicate the things I see," Caroline says. "Because one of the things that makes me feel so helpless is seeing the picture a certain way and feeling like so few people see it that way—and that if they did, things would be different."

Capital defense is in many ways about trying to convey the picture one has seen. Defense teams investigate their clients' lives and histories and try to write that up in a way that will, among other things, communicate the individual's complexity and humanity. Yet as Caroline is saying, the constraints of the legal format or approach can leave attorneys feeling frustratingly unable to communicate fully the breadth and depth of what they have seen.

"We learn so much, and we write it," Caroline continues, "but I really don't think people read it, or the people who do read it are so unaffected by it—the judges and clerks, they have such biases. So it makes me want to figure out some other way to express what I feel and what I see, other than through the legal system."

"What I feel and what I see," I repeat. "I wonder if you can unpack that—what would that be?"

"The humanity in our clients," Caroline answers, tears in her voice. "The struggles that their families suffer, both before and after. I guess it's just helping people understand human beings and human frailties and having some compassion and then making things better."

There is in Caroline's wish both hope and sadness, innovation and frustration—as there is, it seems to me, in all the attorneys' discussions about quitting or otherwise changing the ways in which they engage in capital defense. On the one hand, their speculations or descriptions about getting out of the work—the fantasizing, the re-evaluating, the acknowledgment of the toll the work inevitably takes—are as clear an indication as any of the effect that capital defense has on the people who engage in it day after day. Yet at the same time, it is in these stretches of our conversations that I first begin to hear notes of self-preservation—which is to say, a recognition of the value of protecting not just their clients' lives but their own.

CHAPTER 10

# Staying In

"THERE'S THIS SENSE of urgency, this very deep kind of human response," Lou explains as he describes what it feels like to have a client under death warrant. He is one of the attorneys who likens it to the experience of seeing someone tied to the tracks as a train approaches, adding, "Your human reaction is to try to save them."

It's an instinctive response, Lou says. If you're there, and you see it happening, and perhaps moreover if you have been specifically trained in how to respond to such things, you let the urgency propel you toward the scene, and you try to do what you can.

"But then," Lou continues, "If the train gets too close, you have to get out of the way."

*Yes*, I think to myself. This is what you come to if you extend the vivid image of the onrushing train and the desperate effort to get the individual out of harm's way. This is the next frame of the scene.

"It's kind of like your emotional survival," Lou says. "When you *know* it's going to happen, when it's inevitable, you dive for cover, because you have to survive to go on to the next one."

Later I found myself thinking about the judgment required for the self-preservation Lou describes. Trying feverishly to untie the knots, the rescuer has to determine just when the moment of impossibility has arrived and then have the physical and emotional reflexes to dive for cover. Of course, in actual experience judgments about self-preservation happen not in a split second but over time. But the parallel still seems apt. Given how dedicated they are to the rescue effort and how urgently they feel its pull, where do these capital defenders find shelter when their own survival is at stake? Or—to phrase it less in terms of split-second immediacy and more in terms of their long-term endurance—how do they *keep* preserving themselves so that they are able to survive and carry on over the course of their lives and careers?

Lou frames the issue in terms of being able to "go on to the next one" and continue trying to save people. When he tells me about choosing not to witness clients' executions, he says speculatively, "Maybe that's like turning away when the train comes." Preserving oneself, in this sense, means preserving one's ability to keep engaging in the work. Several of the attorneys talk about focusing their energy on the next task, the next client who needs their attention. I can see this as a healthy response: turn from the dead to continue to fight for the living. Yet as Julian suggests in Chapter 9 when he talks about pouring himself immediately into the next urgent task, it can also be an unsustainable re-channeling of energy that doesn't leave enough time for grief or recovery. If attorneys' emphasis is on persevering, are they protecting their ability to get up the next day and fight for somebody else, or are they ignoring their own needs by forging ahead without respite or acknowledgment? Where is the line between a sustaining and a destructive kind of perseverance?

It's not an easy question, and it gets even harder when the prospect of "the next one" feels not only inspiring but also traumatizing. The urgency of the next client's need can galvanize attorneys' energy and propel them into work on days when they might otherwise be mired in exhaustion and grief—or the encounter with that next client can trigger paralyzing memories of those who are gone. It's hard to predict which reaction will be paramount.

Lou talks about diving for cover so that he will be around to struggle on behalf of the next person on the tracks; he also talks about turning away to protect himself from the sight of the oncoming train. At this level, the distinction between fighting for others and fighting for oneself can blur. Over and over the attorneys say, "It's not about me," continually mindful that they are neither the center of the story nor the ones in most obvious peril. Yet I think Lou gets at something crucial when he observes that if he didn't dive for cover, he wouldn't be around to fight for anyone else. The image is as true emotionally as it is literally. Lou may not be the one tied to the tracks, but if he is too thrown by the impact of the train, he won't be any good to anyone else—not the next person in need, not his family, and not himself. It's the dilemma of anyone who dedicates himself to saving others: self-preservation is arguably not a luxury but a necessity, even if only because it helps maintain one's ability to save. Or because those in the business of lifesaving actually deserve to consider their own lives too. Whatever the reasoning, figuring out how to take care of oneself and keep going is not an extraneous challenge; it's essential.

In Chapter 2, Julian uses the parable of the good Samaritan to describe his own motivation for working as a capital defender. Talking about the compelling pull of the wounded traveler in the ditch and the Samaritan's unwillingness to pass by, Julian says, "There's a sense of urgency that these kinds of situations have always engendered in me. There's something in me that refuses to pass by."

This defining characteristic of Julian's approach to the world hasn't altered over the years, I'd venture to guess, but he has become better acquainted with his own limits and more adept at figuring out the range of possible ways to respond to what he sees. He reflects on this as we speak.

"You can say, I have the capacity to do this, but maybe somebody else is better," he begins, "Or you can say, I've reached my limit, so although I have the capacity, in some ways I don't, because I can't handle something anymore, so there is a choice—oftentimes there is a choice—to figure out how to respond."

Julian implies that you can define capacity literally, in terms of ability, but you can also define it in terms of physical and emotional tolerance. Once the question becomes not only "What is my capacity?" but also

"What does it take from me to act on that capacity time and time again?" the answers may vary.

"I'm able to step back a bit and get some perspective that I didn't have before," Julian says now. "I'm able to realize there are places I shouldn't go because I have to preserve myself. I have much better perspective than I used to have, to know that sometimes if I'm the Samaritan walking by, maybe I should just dial 911 as opposed to doing CPR."

As hard as it can be to accept that there are limits—of one's own capacity and of the feasibility of the task in the first place—some measure of acceptance can also be a relief, if the attorneys can manage to feel it. Julian's recognition of his own limits lets him imagine alternate approaches. And placing that recognition within a broader context—acknowledging that there are limits to what *anyone* can do—can help guard against too much self-blame.

"I feel like I have a little more perspective [now]," Gabe tells me, "in that I can say, It's OK if you can't change this because [this eminent attorney] couldn't change it either. It's sort of knowing what your limitations are and understanding that you can't fix everything."

It's about knowing what your own personal limitations are, but also about recognizing the situation's inherent limitations. Gabe, it seems, is talking about both.

"I'm sure it happens to oncologists," he speculates, "that someone comes in with cancer you can't cure because it's too far advanced. [The death penalty] is very different—it's not an organic process that's killing the person—but maybe it's similar in that you have to realize your limitations. Getting perspective over time may have helped me deal with things that might have at one time felt like failures. I don't know if that's a rationalization, but it feels like perspective."

It's interesting to consider the difference between rationalization and perspective. We tend to speak as if rationalization involves talking oneself into something that is not necessarily true, whereas perspective involves genuine recognition of the truth. Yet with so much that is at issue here—feeling for and heeding one's own limits, for example, or determining what is and is not one's own fault—the emotional reality of the experience is influenced by the story we are able to tell ourselves about it. When I hear Gabe and others describe a process of gaining greater perspective, I hear them talking about their efforts to understand the story of the life-saving battle they are engaged in—and specifically how to view their own role in it.

Attorneys who have been practicing this high-stakes, high-intensity law for many years have in fact developed ways of sustaining themselves and persevering, even as they are also hurting in ways that they may not fully acknowledge or address. Engaging in capital defense for ten, twenty, even thirty years, as they have, means they have learned something about self-preservation and endurance, whether or not they consciously set out to learn it.

"I think one of the few healthy things that I do is run a lot," says Nick. "I'll put headphones on and go out and run for two hours. It clears my head. That's one of the things that allows me to stay [in this work]."

It's so simple on the face of it, and yet so important in light of all the comments in Chapter 9 about the toll the work takes on the attorneys' physical selves. It can be hard to convince overworked professionals with enormous demands on their time that taking time out for their own health or rejuvenation would actually be a way to serve the goal of helping others, and indeed Nick is critical of what he perceives as the self-indulgence of taking *too* much time off from work. But a run in the middle of the day, a break he can take anywhere and come back refreshed, is something he allows himself and something that he views as contributing to his ability to sustain this kind of work for so long.

An ongoing challenge, though, is that the things they often feel too busy for are also the things that the attorneys find most restorative. If this is sometimes true of physical exercise or sleep or travel, it seems especially true of time with their families. As we saw in Chapter 3, the tension that arises when one must choose between writing an urgent legal pleading and spending time with the family can be enormous and not easily resolved.

"You do come to accept: I have to be able to live my life," says Karen after talking about these challenges. "I have to be able to take care of my child, if I'm going to do this work long-term." It's a continual struggle, she says, both practically and sometimes emotionally too. Karen worries about how her "exhaustion, distraction, and depression" affects her parenting during the intense days of work on a client's case.

"But [my daughter] is the first person I want to see after an execution," she says with quiet emphasis. "I try not to feel burdensome. I don't *tell* her that, but—she's the first person I want to see."

For all the additional demands that they place on the attorneys who are parents, children also offer a kind of life-affirming antidote to the death penalty work. The attorneys express both appreciation and concern about this; the concern is about the kind of overburdening that Karen says she tries to avoid. Although their children can do so much to replenish them, these attorneys say they don't want to burden their children by relying on them to serve that function.

"When I'm involved in a case and I hear a story of deprivation and heartbreak, you know what that makes me want to do?" Tim asks rhetorically. "Go home and be with my kids, hug my kids, play games with my kids." As hard as Tim works, his clients' stories not only arouse in him a desire to advocate on *their* behalf; they also drive him home by making acute his awareness of the impact of deprivation on children's lives.

"Of course," Tim laughs, "I try not to overreact to it, but—OK, let's start at home. Let's show my kids first that they're loved."

Like Karen, Tim doesn't want to overreact in turning to his kids, but he does want to act on the impulse to be with them. Gina speaks similarly as she talks about the impact of investigating her clients' life histories. "In some ways, I think [this work] has made me a better parent," she says. "Everything we learn about the effects of not meeting your children's needs becomes real. In some weird sense I feel like it makes me a better parent because I realize what the effects are."

Children have enormous needs, and clients have enormous needs. While the combination is no doubt sometimes overwhelming, it also seems from some attorneys' comments that one set of needs can feel like a counterweight for the other. "In a sense," Paul reflects, "Children [are] an anchor away from the work. [When they were young] they deserved and needed a great deal from me and called it forth—in probably a way that may have been sort of therapeutic for me."

Part of what may make family life feel so therapeutic is that it's a reminder of the world beyond the death penalty. "What helps?" I ask Roger after he vividly describes the depression that he feels in the weeks following a client's execution.

"Going back to all the things I like, things I didn't do during that time," he answers readily. "Going running with my dogs, playing soccer with my kids. You know, one thing this work does for you is it makes you appreciate the little pleasures of life."

On the one hand, the urgency of capital defense can make it hard to yield fully to those ordinary pleasures of life, as so many of the attorneys say in Chapter 3. "How can I do anything else when a life is in my hands?" they wonder. Yet in the aftermath of that heightened urgency, the daily pleasures feel all the more precious.

"This is what life is about!" Roger declares. "This is what makes life good! [An execution] makes you want to go back to that. . . . I think when you're away from [ordinary life], you come to appreciate how valuable and how fulfilling it is."

I think of Karen talking about the feeling of "opposites" that she has after a client's execution: a lack of appetite because she feels guilty for enjoying a good meal but at the same time an acute awareness of the blues and greens of the world around her. Gabe and I share a similar moment of juxtaposition after his interview. I have turned off the recorder, but we are still talking as we walk outside, trading stories from the grim world of the death penalty. Gabe finishes his thought and takes a deep breath.

"Well, it's a beautiful day," he says, as indeed it is. We stand a moment, breathing it in. Is the day a solace or a painful contrast? Capital defenders can walk out of prison or out of grief and be hit with the crushing indifference of the rest of the world: the bright blue sky, the people—like the shoppers walking past Pamela as she sat in the mall that execution night—who have no idea. Capital defenders can feel separate from everyone else because of what they've seen and what they feel. But sometimes, too, they can emerge back into the ordinary world and let it comfort them, let it remind them that they have as much place there as they do in sadness and loss.

"There are lots of moments of joy," Adam says as we conclude our interview, "and we've got to recognize them, appreciate them, and suck all the juice out of them when we get 'em, because they're what keeps us going."

What keeps any of us going? So much depends on where we look and what meaning we make of what we see. "At some level I realized I couldn't keep doing this if I gauged my own success or failure as a lawyer by what happened in these cases," Paul says, reflecting on his many years of work as a capital defender. "At some point," he continues, "you become focused more on what you do and how you do it and less on how it's received by the courts. If you're solely dependent on outcomes, you don't survive the executions. [But if] you focus on the process, on what you do, you get devastated emotionally by how it turns out, but you don't live and die based on that. You live based on the work you do."

As I consider Paul's words, I find myself remembering all the reflections about success and failure, responsibility and fault that the attorneys have explored during our interviews. There is, of course, no single truth about any of this. There are clearly so many ways that the attorneys can and do feel, sometimes all at once. Paul here describes one possible way to experience his role and his inevitable losses—a way that, by his own description, accounts for at least some of what has enabled him to keep engaging in the work for so long. To be able to keep going is, perhaps, to fight for the best outcomes but not stake your entire identity on whether you achieve them. Recalling Merton's words again, not to depend on the hope of results, and yet to persist in hoping.

Paul is clearly not talking about becoming callous or even inured. "You get devastated emotionally by how it turns out," he says, slipping in that phrase even as he is also talking about perspective and coping strategies and endurance. There is perhaps no way around the emotional devastation, no matter how many years of experience an attorney has. "It *should* be hard," Nick said in Chapter 8. But in Paul's words I hear something about the steadying value of focusing on the work itself and, as he says a few moments later, on "the energy and the inspiration and the craft" that it takes to do it.

And within that energy and inspiration and craft is also a surprising privilege: the opportunity to get right into the middle of the fight and do the work that you feel drawn to do, able to do, asked to do, however much you might also rage against the fact of its needing to be done in the first place. Says Isabel at the end of her interview,

> I do think that paths are opened up for you, and you can sort of choose if you follow [them] or not. Rightly or wrongly, this was a path that through a very serendipitous set of circumstances was opened up to me. . . . I certainly didn't go to law school thinking I wanted to be a death penalty lawyer. But I think that people are chosen for things because they can do it. [Capital defense] is not something that everybody can do. It's somewhat a gift and somewhat a curse to be able to do it, and for whatever reason, I was able to.

Though there is much they don't talk about with one another, the immense solidarity and identification with other dedicated and experienced capital defense attorneys is clearly another part of what buttresses and inspires these attorneys over the long haul. "Everybody draws on whatever inner resources they have that help you get through difficult things," Lou says. When I ask him what he draws on, he says, "I think of people who were heroic fighters of power. I realize I'm in a long lineage."

Viewing themselves as fighters and, moreover, viewing themselves as part of a long lineage and a strong community of similar fighters is hugely important. It can be a large part of what draws them into the work in the first place, as we saw in Chapter 2, and it can be a crucial part of what keeps them there.

"The [capital defense] community just has a collection of incredibly gifted, warm, sensitive people," Keith says, "so for most of my life I've been overwhelmed by the people that are in this circle, and I think just being in that circle is a good place to be, and in some ways you don't want to leave."

Keith is speaking of what he would miss if he were to stop doing death penalty work. "What holds me in," he continues, "is a sense of community with other people who have been in the work longer than I have and remain in the work, or some of the people that I was influential in bringing into the work. I mean, a big part of it is I want to stay involved in the work because of the great people I want to stay in fellowship with."

Benjamin expresses similar sentiments. "I like the work, and I love some of my clients," he says, "but ultimately it's about the respect and love that I have for other people who do death penalty defense—that is what keeps me in it. And when I think about not doing it anymore, that's the part I think I would miss the most."

The prospect of missing his colleagues isn't all that binds Benjamin to their shared enterprise, however. He also very specifically feels a sense of "not wanting to let them down" by abandoning the work they are engaged in together. "It becomes like being in a foxhole," he says. "You don't want to be the one who lets down the other person who is counting on you."

Benjamin speaks of not wanting to opt out before he has fulfilled his obligations—to his clients and to his colleagues. Others expresses a variation on this idea when they talk about wanting to stick around until the death penalty is finally abolished—as if they feel themselves to be part of that effort and don't want to miss the ending if it were to happen within their lifetimes. "That's part of it," Simon admits as he brings this up. "Just hanging on! I keep thinking we're going to let go of [the death penalty], and I want to be there when that happens."

Like so many of the attorneys' deeply held feelings, this too has its counterweight, seemingly opposite but equally acute. Not long after expressing this desire to stick it out until he can witness some kind of better ending, Simon talks about wanting to go backward.

"The experience I keep having," he says, "and I've had this feeling in the situations you were asking about, when I've just lost a client—is wishing I could go back, and indeed almost doing it, transporting myself, just to try to let go of what I'm dealing with."

He pauses, and I ask him to say more about the wish. "Is it to go back to an earlier time of life? Is that what the wish is for?"

"No, I actually do it," he corrects me. "I let myself just go there for a minute and pretend like I don't know any of this."

What I first heard only as an expression of longing I now understand to be the description of a strategy, a kind of internal diving for cover that he has figured out how to create for himself.

"What does that give you—kind of a relief, a reprieve?" I ask, just to confirm it.

He nods. "It's like going to sleep, where you can let go or just be away from it—"

He breaks off, his voice thick with emotion. I feel all of it now: the ingeniousness of the coping strategy and the longing that has given rise to it.

After a moment Simon continues, "I find myself in these really difficult moments wanting to go back, wanting to go home, not just physically but mentally. I want this all not to have happened. I want it not to have happened to my clients. I want for me not to have learned what it really is."

As I have felt during so many moments throughout the interviews, I am left with awe at the strength and the fragility of human beings, both at once. As I sit with Simon, I marvel at the mind's ability to dive for cover and give itself at least a temporary protection or respite. I appreciate the range of survival strategies that are there for the taking (or the creating). Yet at the same moment, I feel the impact of what Simon has come to know and the awareness that he can never truly not know it or be unaffected by it. There is no real going back, yet there is sometimes in human beings a startling ability to reclaim, to give ourselves whatever we most crave, which Simon's momentary transporting of himself so vividly exemplifies.

Strength and fragility: this duality is present in all the interviews. Are these attorneys vulnerable enough to be deeply, even irrevocably affected by what they have experienced? Yes. Are they resilient enough to have found all manner of ways to carry on? Absolutely.

If they have up to now talked less about the fragility, it may be because they fear they cannot have one and also the other, cannot be both unable and able to tolerate the stress and grief of their work, cannot be knocked down and yet also capable of getting up to keep fighting. What I learned from them, though, and what I hold back up to them through these words, is that it is exactly possible to be both, feel both, do both.

# Epilogue

A FEW WEEKS after I completed my final set of interviews, I attended a national conference where a well-known capital defense attorney was the keynote speaker. I had heard him before and knew what an elegant and powerful rhetorician he is.

That morning, he took the podium after the expected laudatory introduction. He began to speak but then faltered and fell silent. The room was silent, too, as the audience grasped that he was not pausing for emphasis or effect. After a long couple of moments, he gathered himself enough to continue. With an apology, he explained that a client had been executed the night before—in other words, just a few hours ago. He was feeling a little shaky, he said, and hadn't been sure he would make it to the conference in time to give this talk.

Regaining his familiar momentum and verbal elegance, he went on to weave an account of this recent experience into a searing talk about the death penalty. He spoke with breathtaking clarity about brokenness—the system's, his clients', and also, he said, his own. He described his final phone conversation with this recent client, during which the man had thanked him for what he'd tried to do.

I couldn't stop crying, even as I rose with the others around me to give him a standing ovation. It was the impact of the talk itself but also the timing of it, so immediately in the aftermath of the client's execution and, for me, so immediately in the aftermath of a year of listening to capital defenders describe exactly this shakiness. I felt as if this public audience had been given a glimpse of the private suffering I had been witnessing in interview after interview over the past months.

When I think back on it now, it's the juxtapositions that are so moving to me: The attorney's private grief momentarily visible on a public stage. His doubt about his ability to get up and do the next thing and his doing it anyway, getting on a plane to go where he had been asked to go. The challenge of standing in front of others and being looked to for clarity and guidance when he was feeling so exhausted and unsteady. The way he faltered, without words, and then found words to speak so eloquently of what he had experienced. I am guessing that he wanted to speak to us about the circumstances of his client's life—right up to their phone conversation the night before—that would not be reported in the news. I am assuming that he wanted to tell that story, to have us feel its impact.

And listening to him, hearing in my mind the echoes of twenty other attorneys' interviews, remembering each unique balance of faltering and eloquence, I knew that part of the story this attorney was telling was his own. Part of the impact of last night's execution was on him.

The death penalty is in so many ways about the worst that human beings can do to one another. So many of its tragedies feel both horrific and unnecessary, so that one is left simultaneously with a sense of obligation and a sense of waste: so much compelling need and so much human energy going toward carrying out, or trying to avert, a life-taking event that arguably never has to happen at all.

Capital defenders enter this story as attorneys who are also, by their own descriptions, something like oncologists or social workers or lifeguards. Their work is often tedious and protracted; they pursue leads in extensive investigations of their clients' lives and file highly technical legal pleadings, persisting with litigation that may take months and even years. Yet at the core of capital defense is a sense of urgency and the "very deep kind of human response" that Lou described.

At the end of George Dennison's novel *Shawno*, a group of men are running through snowy woods to help a neighbor who has fallen gravely ill. "Something priceless was visible in their faces," the narrator recounts, "and I have been moved by the recollection of it again and again. It was the purified, electric look of wholehearted response" (New York: Schocken, 1984, 62).

I've thought often of that image as I've spent hour after hour with capital defense attorneys. Like Dennison's narrator, I've been moved again and again by the need these men and women recognize, the urgency it arouses in them, the wholehearted response they deliver. *You're called upon to do extraordinary things sometimes*, said Gabe. *It's extraordinary work that needs to be done*, said Karen. Here is one more paradox of this extraordinary work: I wish it didn't need to be done; I marvel at whatever it is in human beings that can do it, that will do it.

And after the response, after the adrenaline recedes, there is something else that is also visible: the impact. What these capital defenders are left with and what they now carry—the abiding sadness, the weight, the shakiness, the nightmares, the self-doubt, the alienation, the rage, the helplessness. Unlike disease or natural disaster, the death penalty is not something that just happens. It's something we decide to do. For exactly that reason, its impact deserves our fullest attention.

# INDEX